# The Exciting Easter Coloring book

## A Fun Easter Coloring Book for Kids of All Ages

By Dexter Jacobs

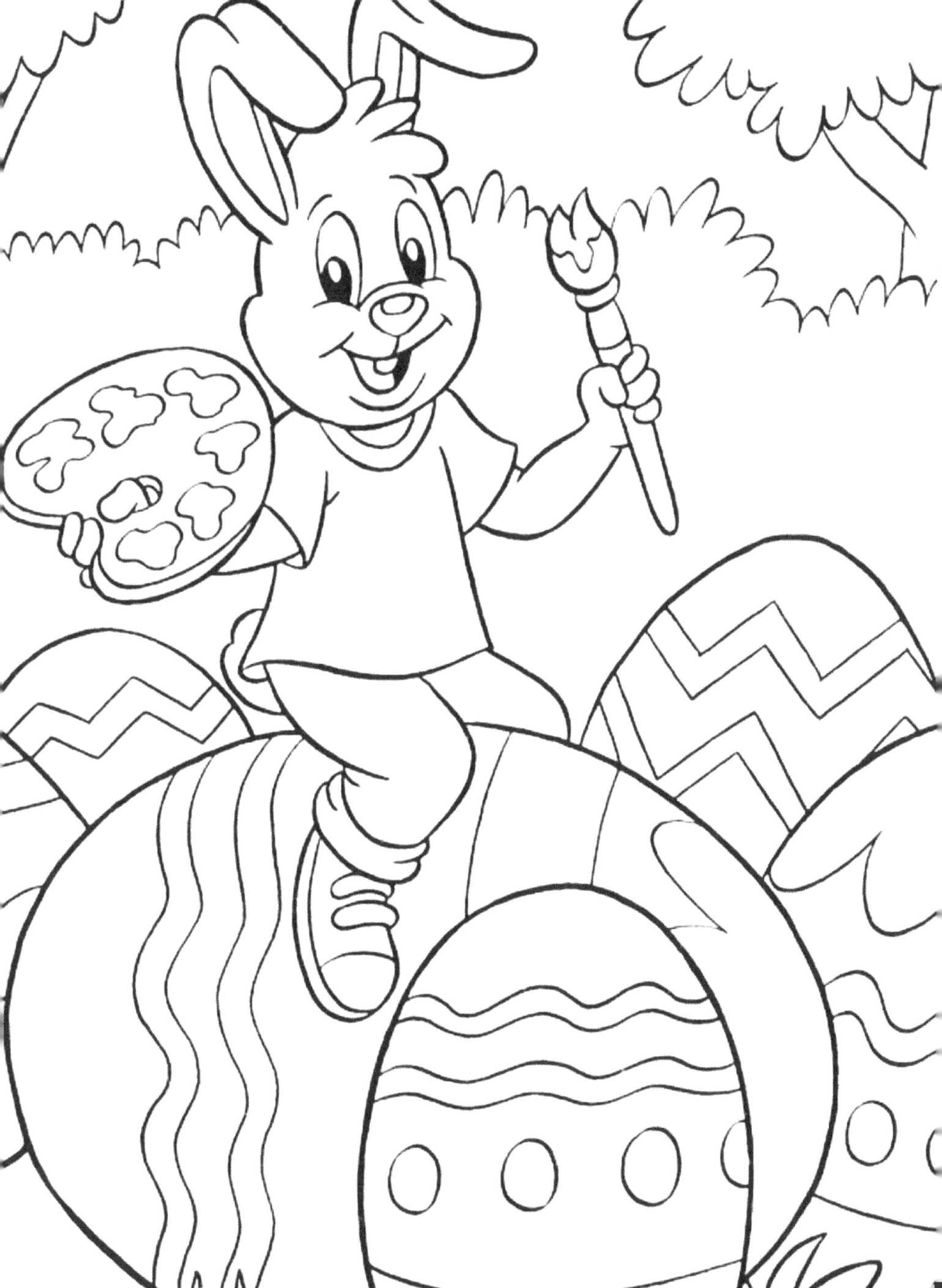

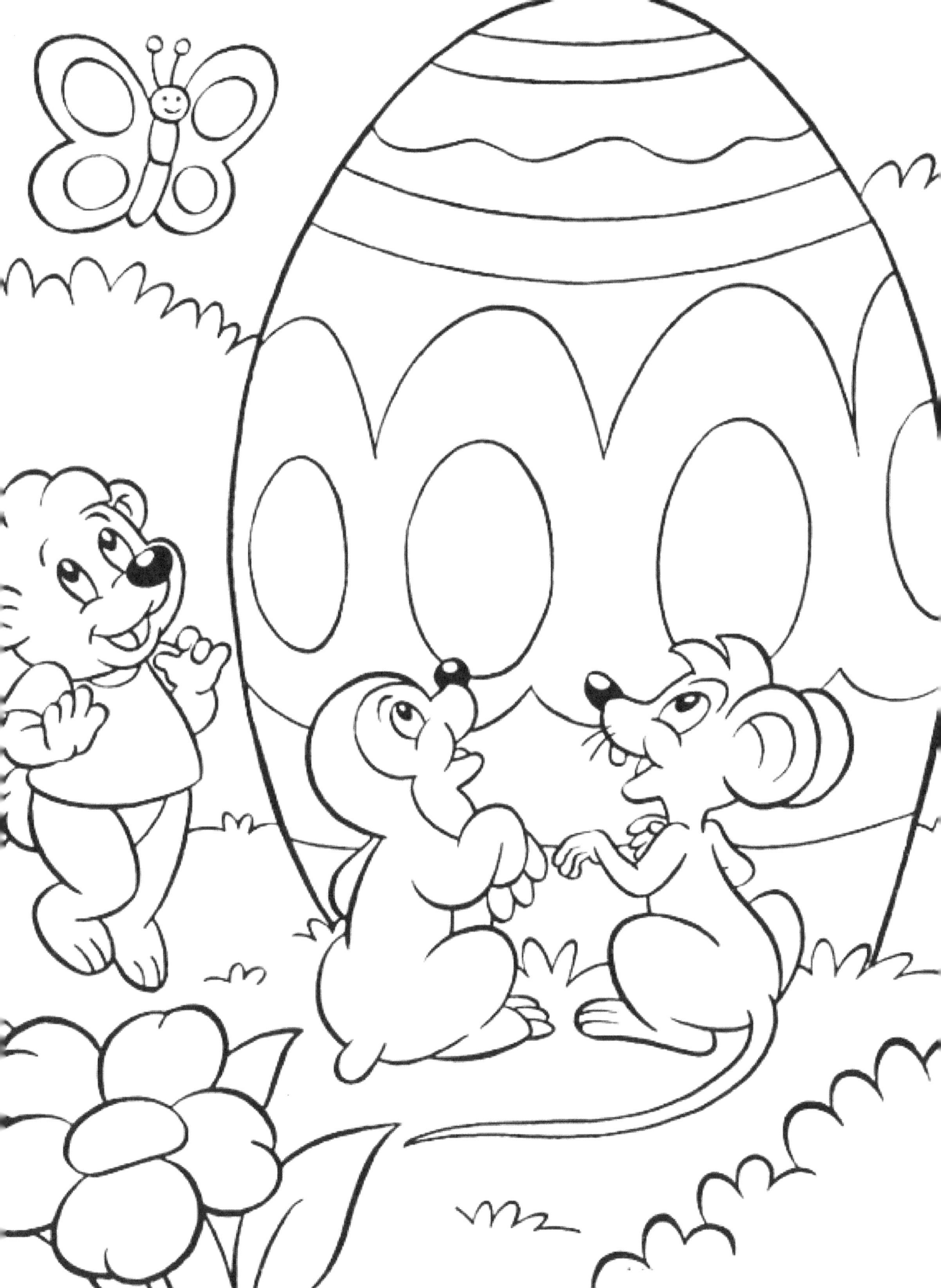

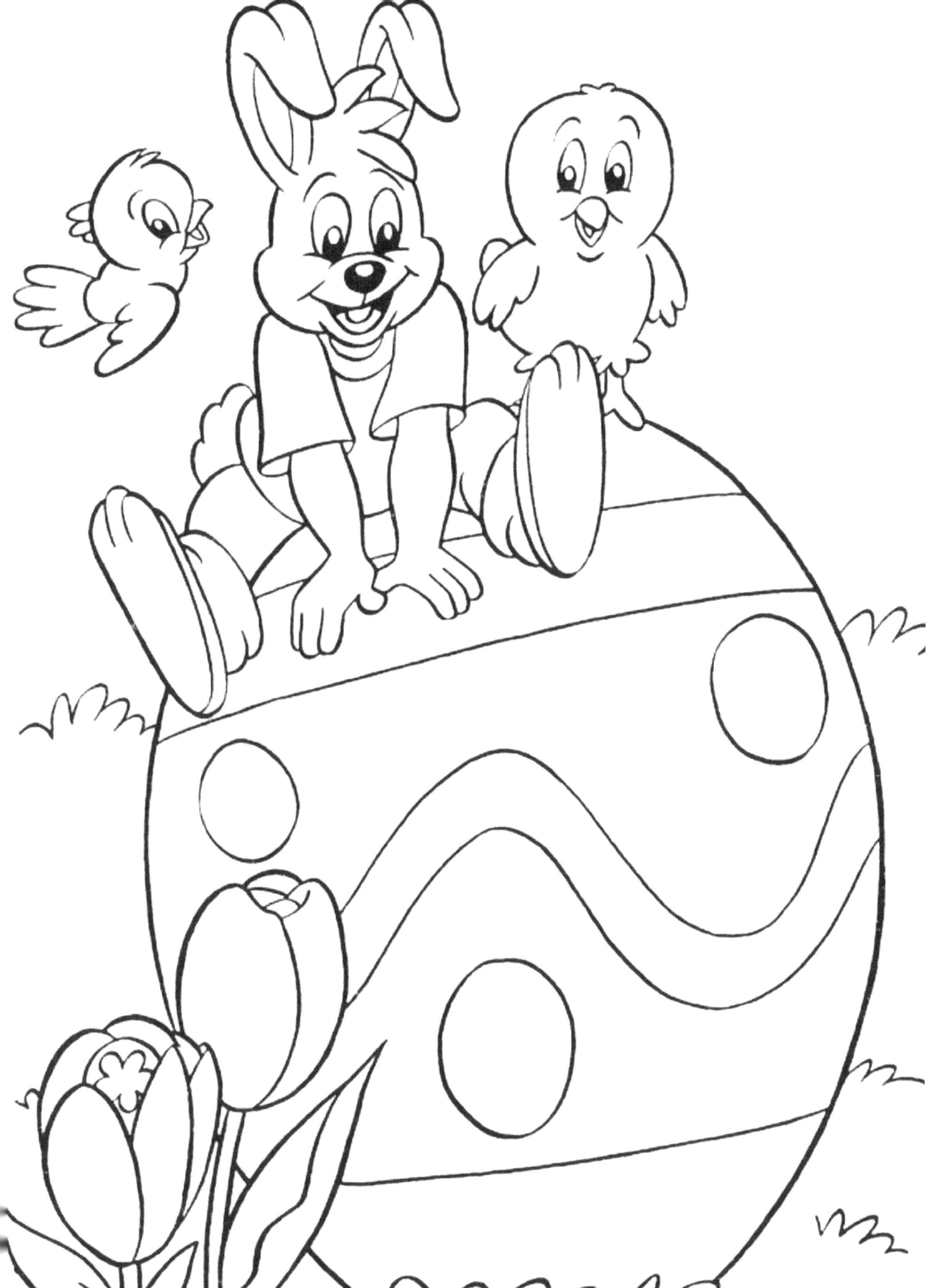

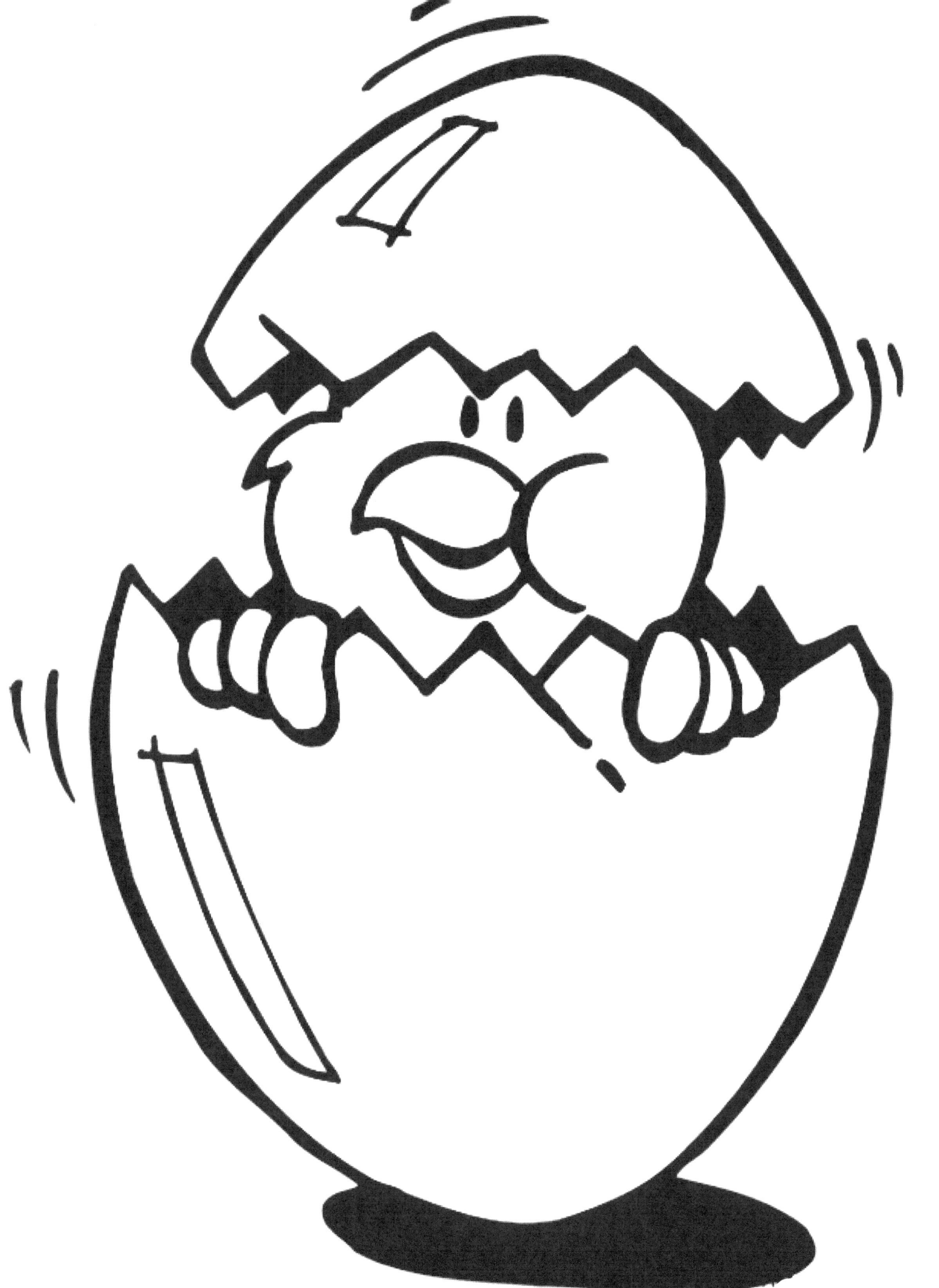

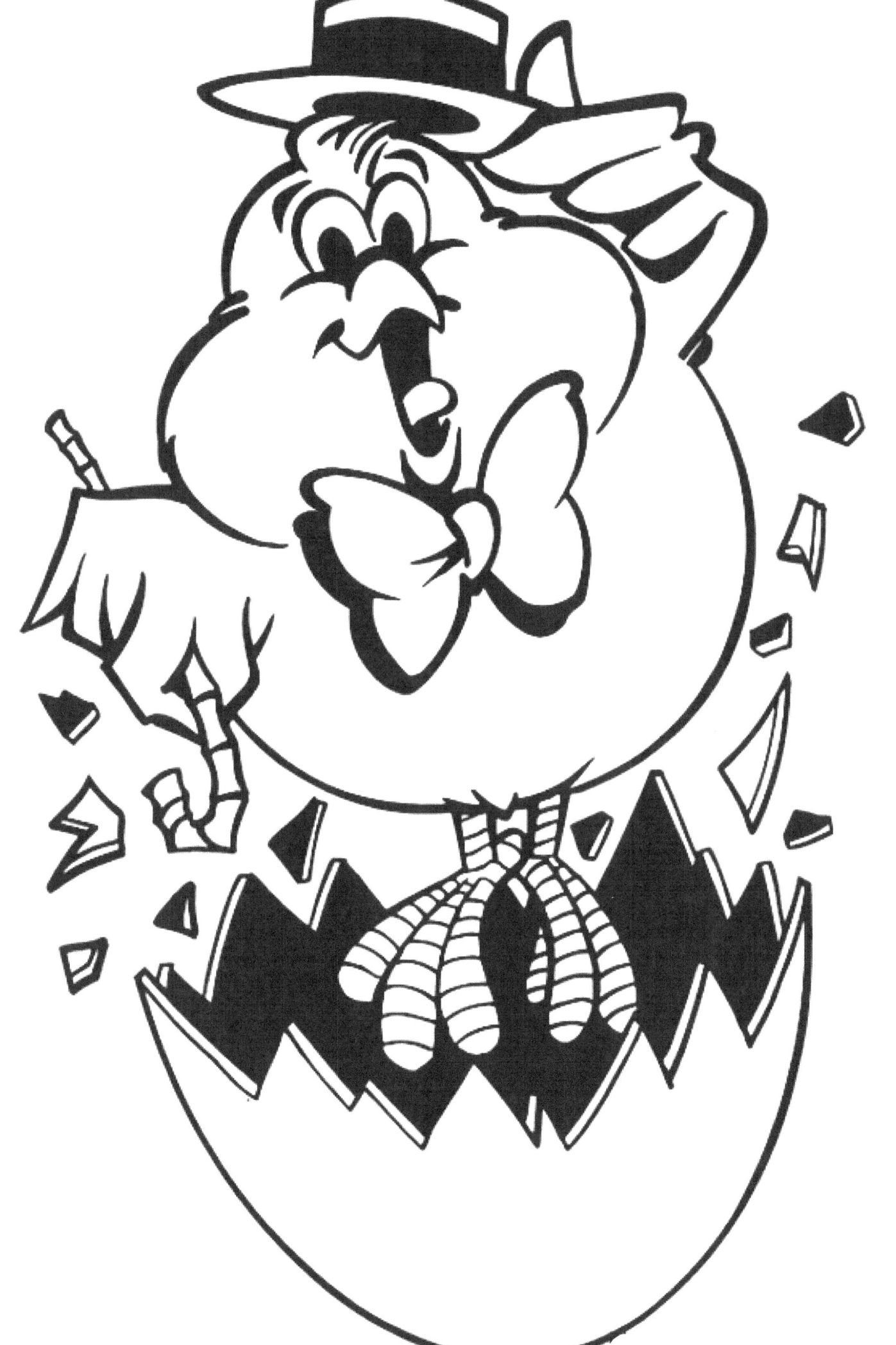

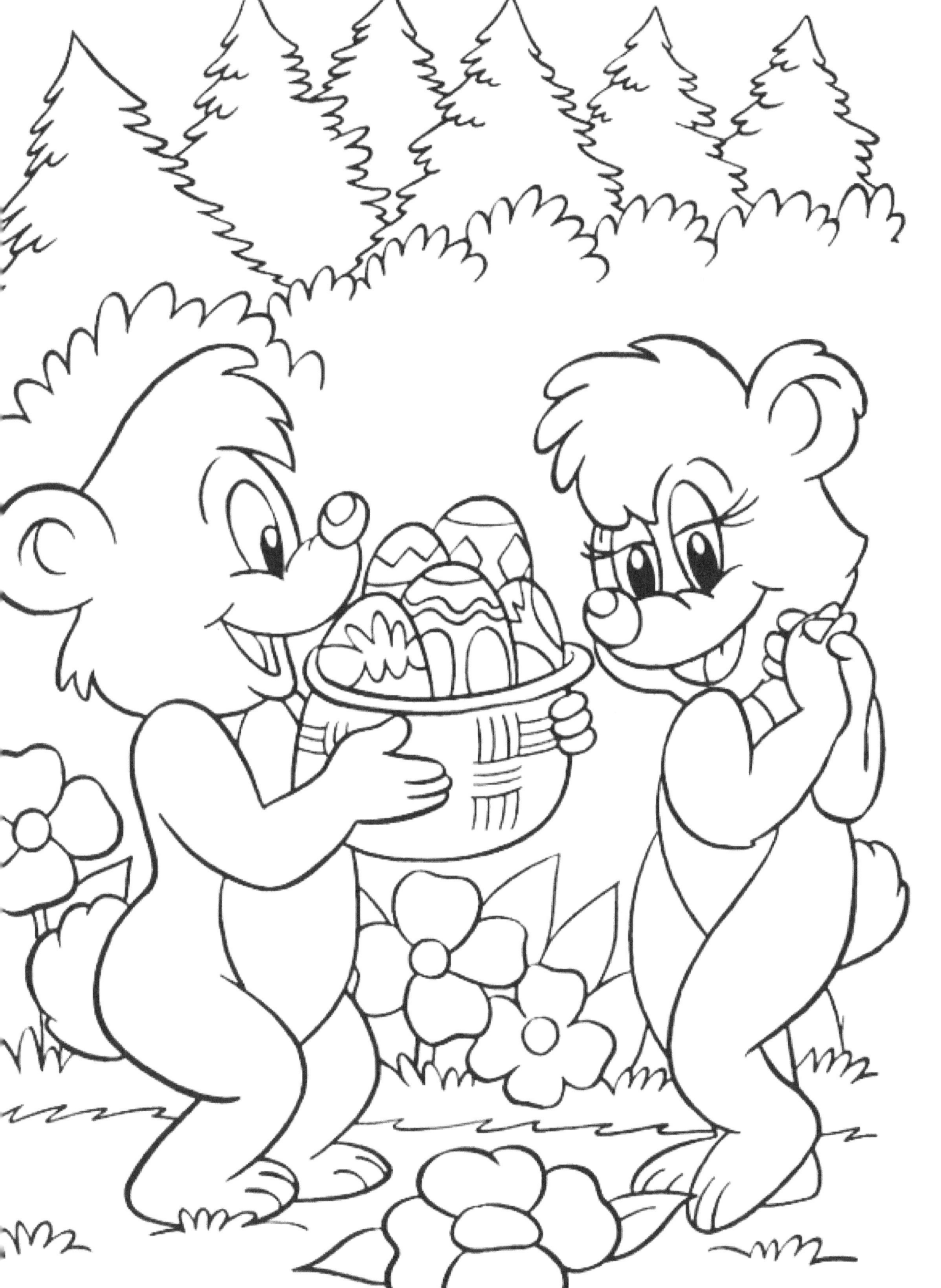

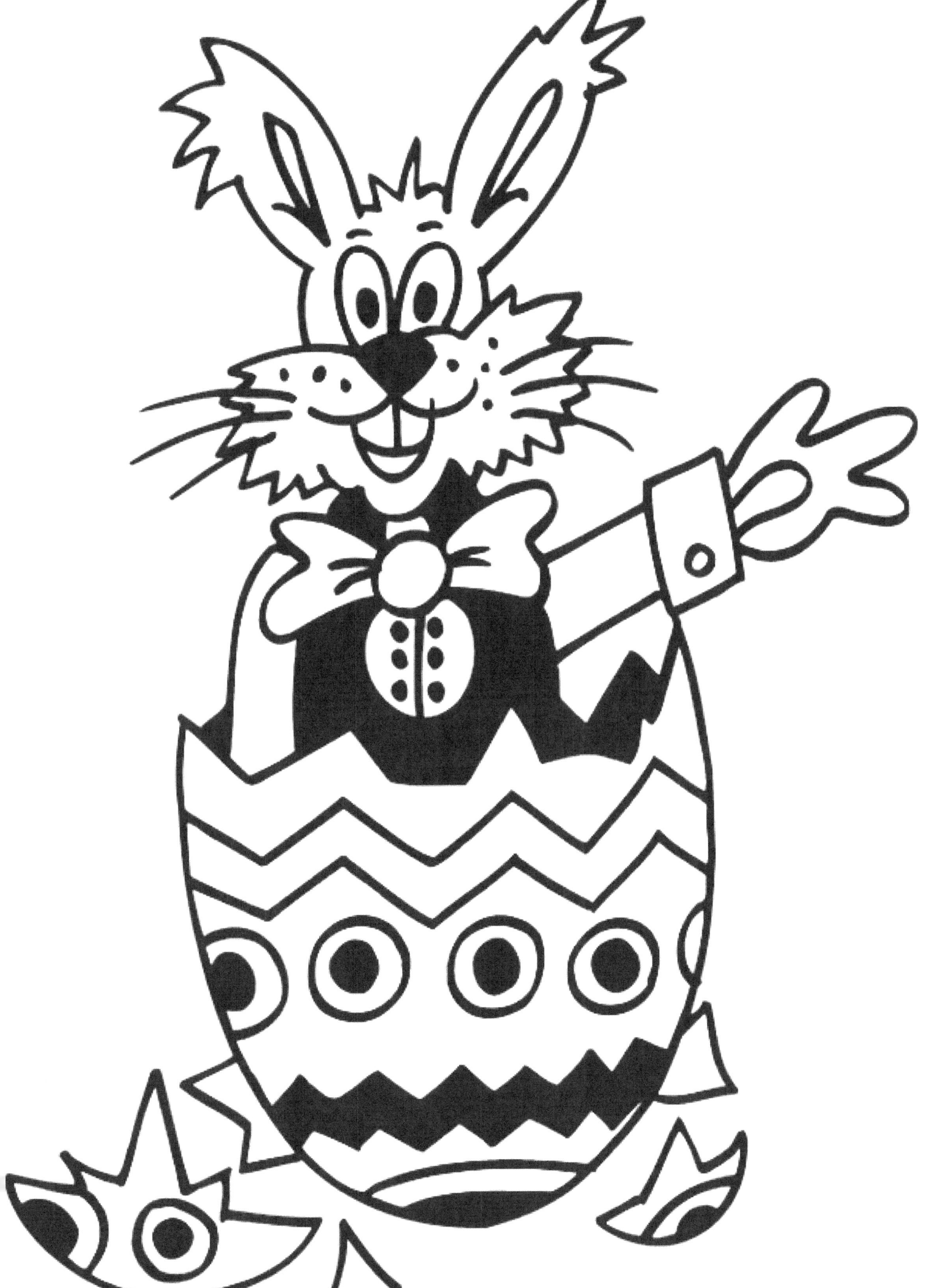

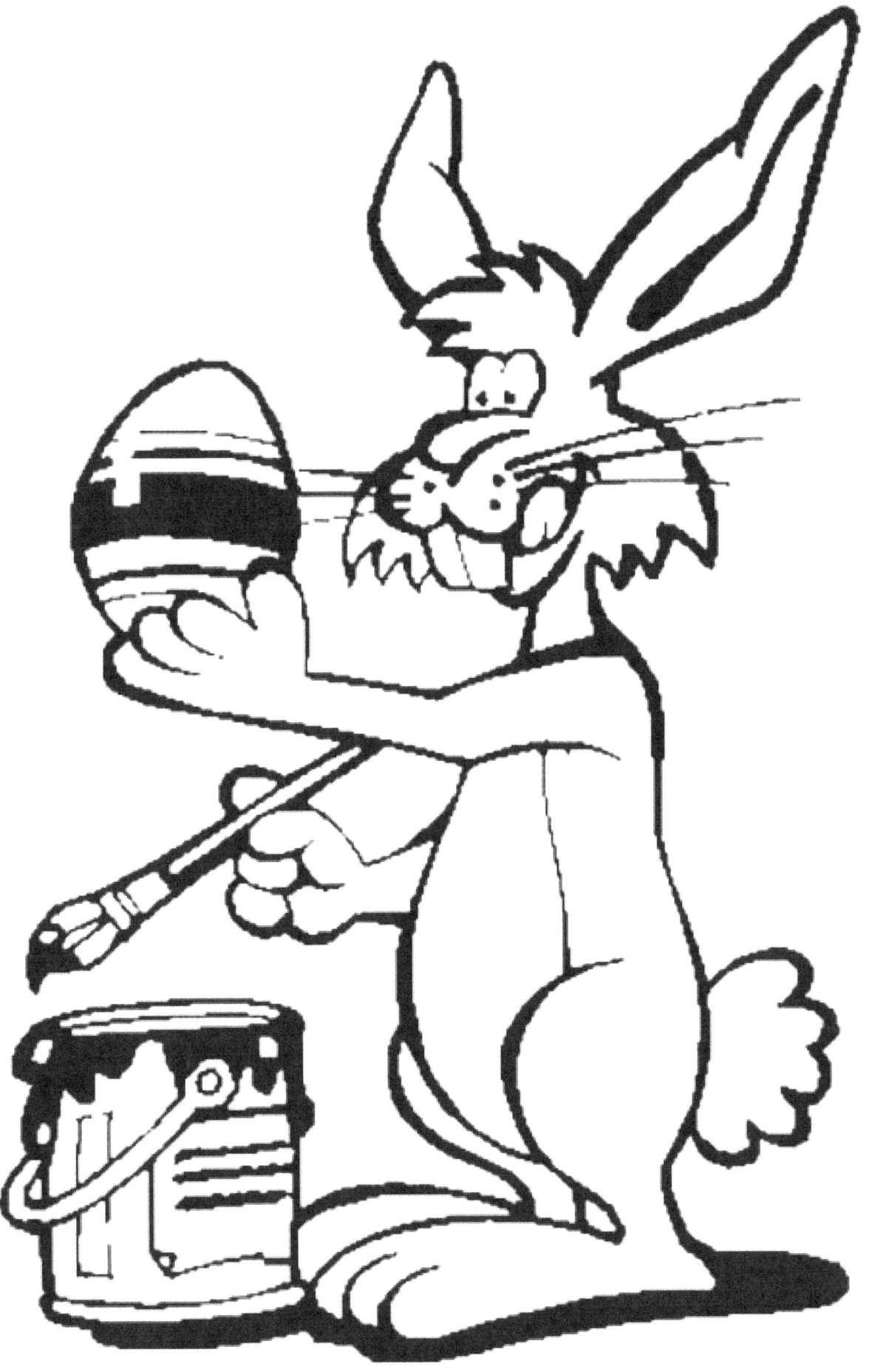

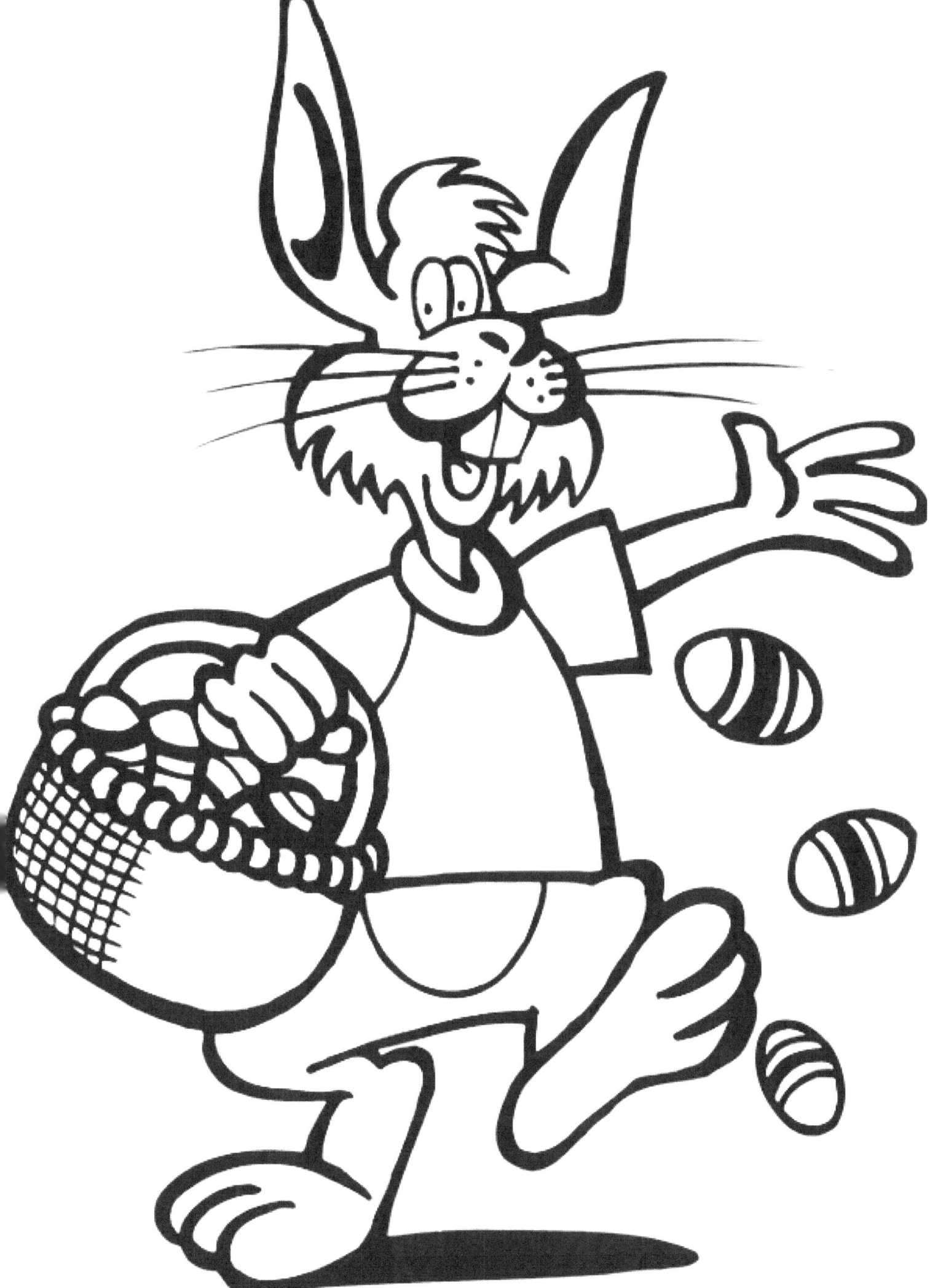

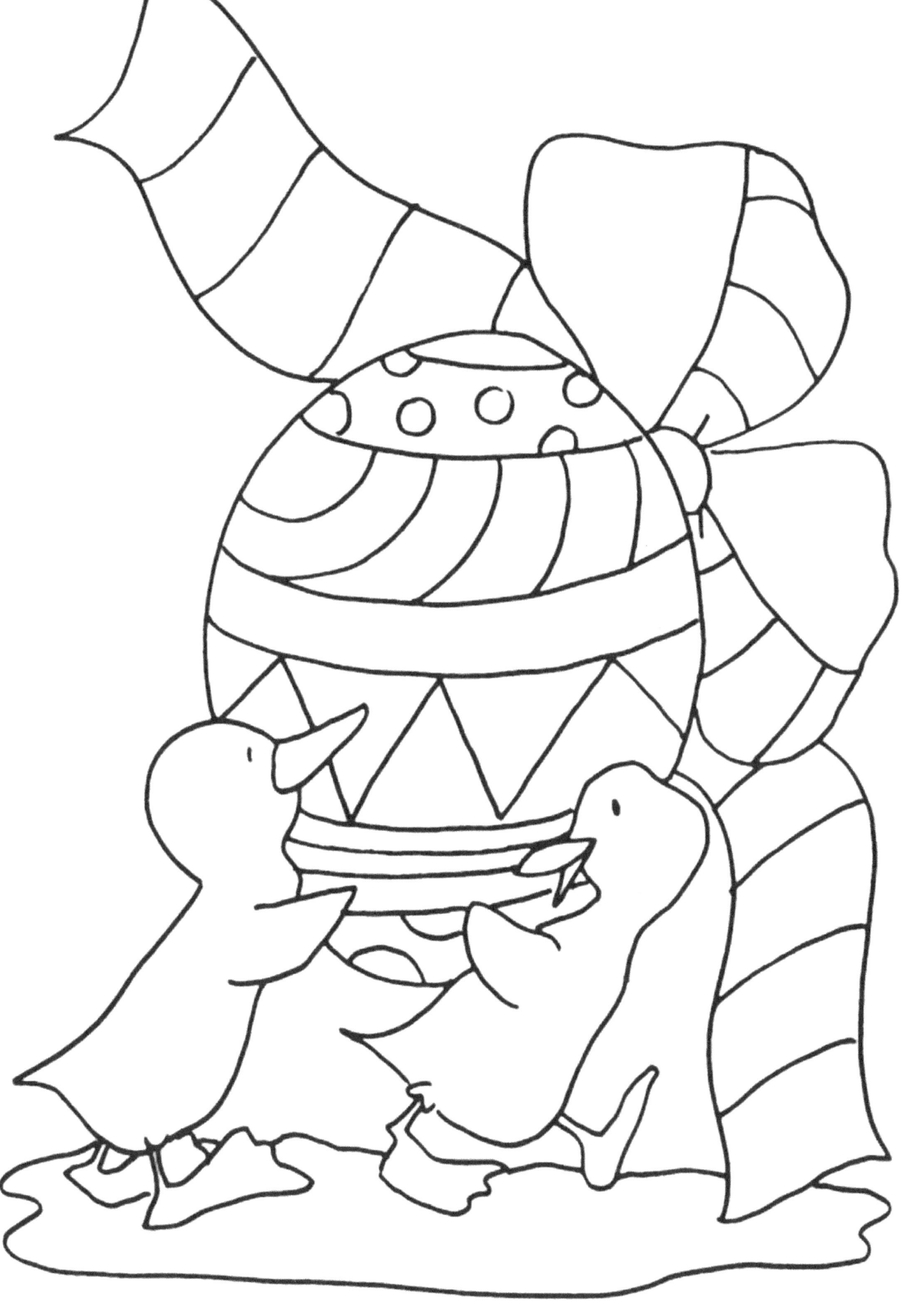

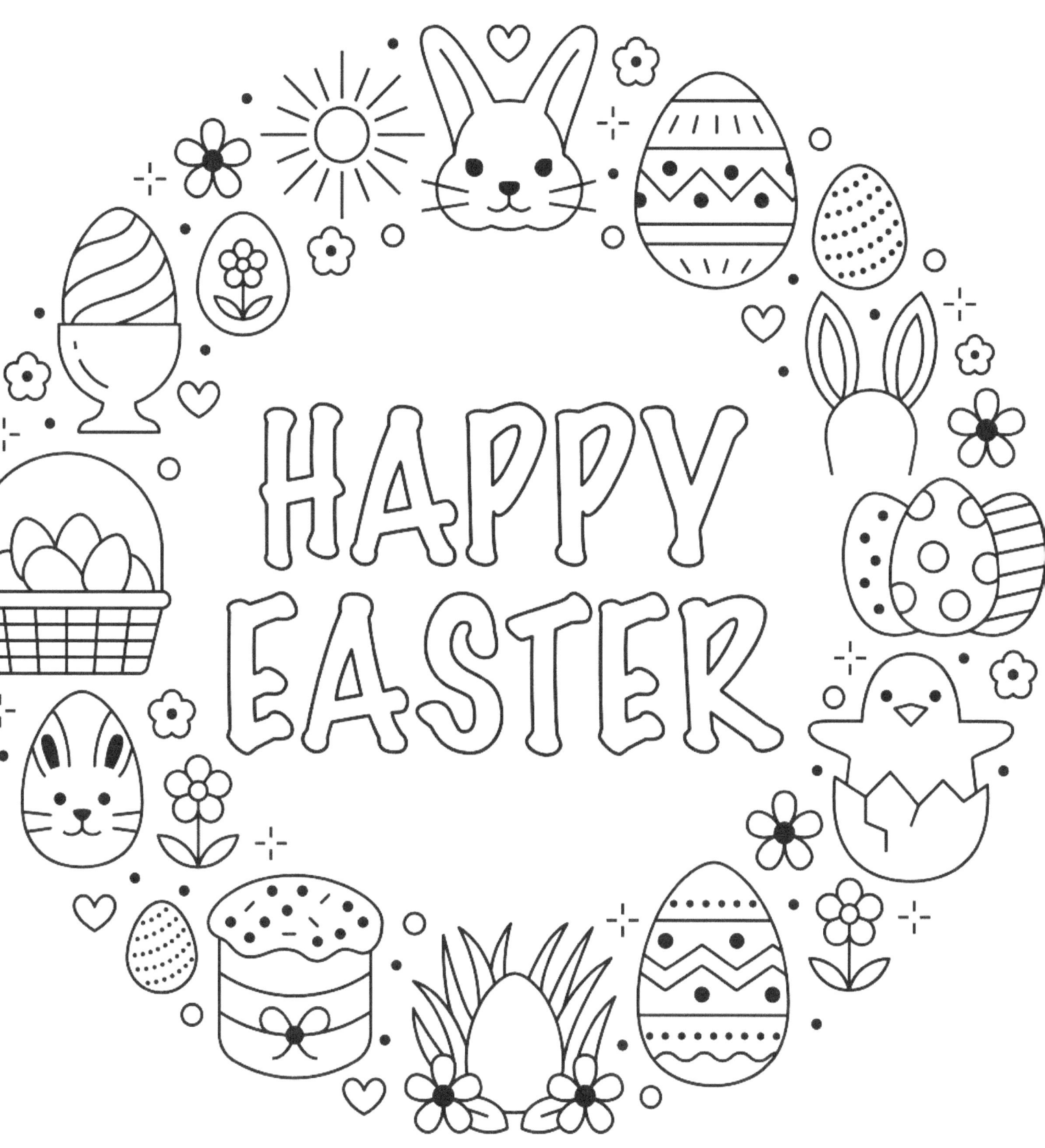

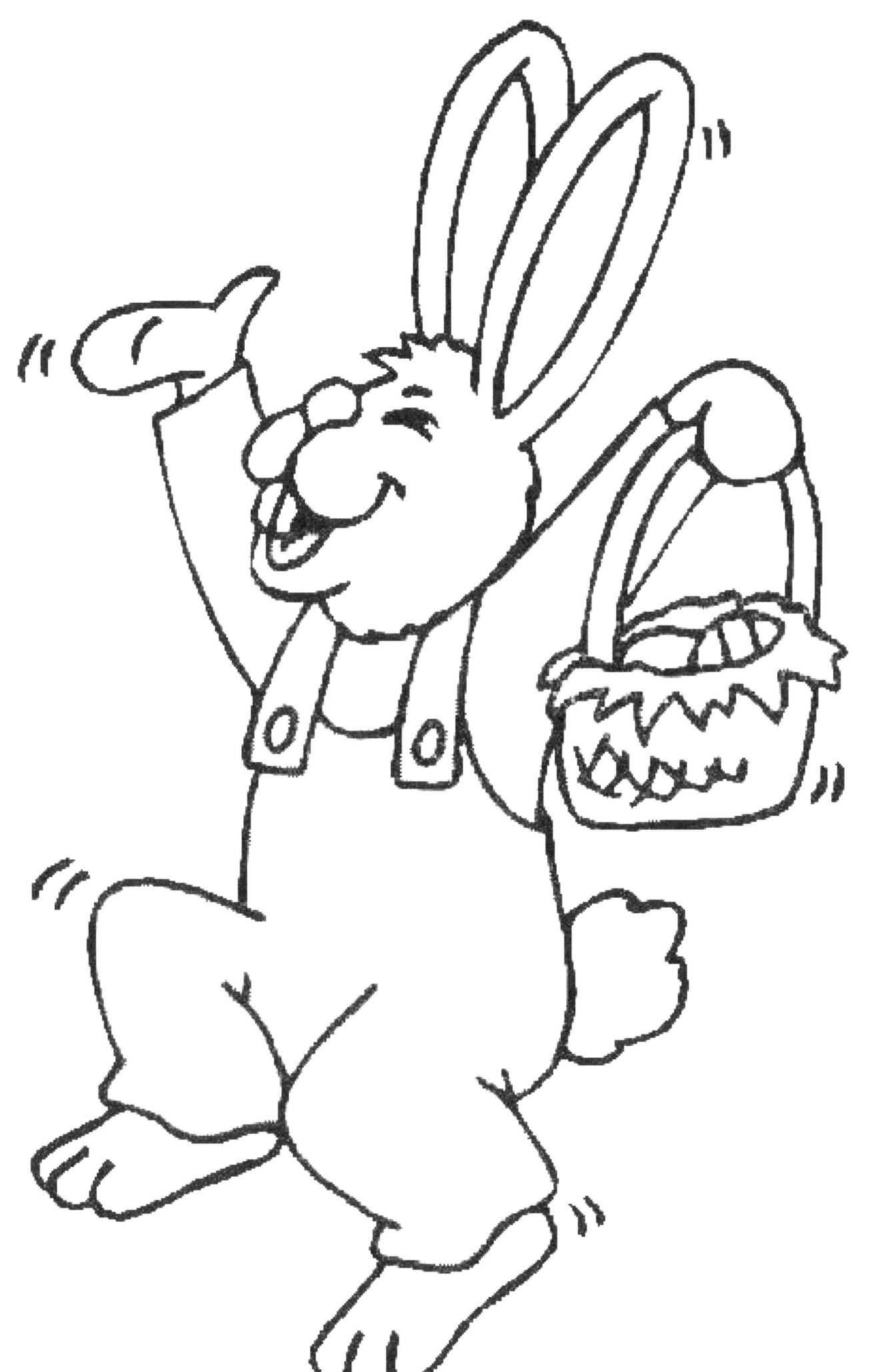

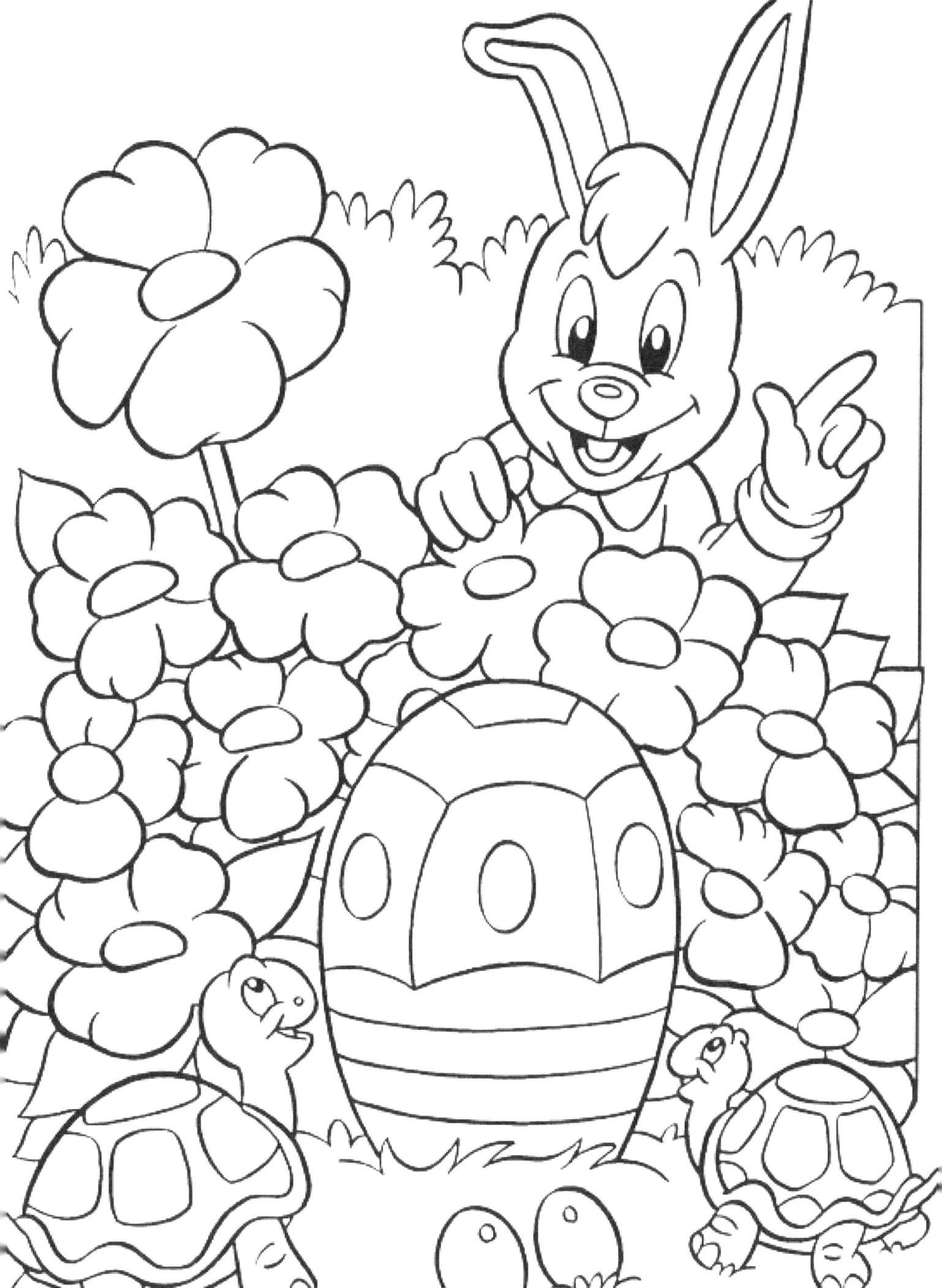

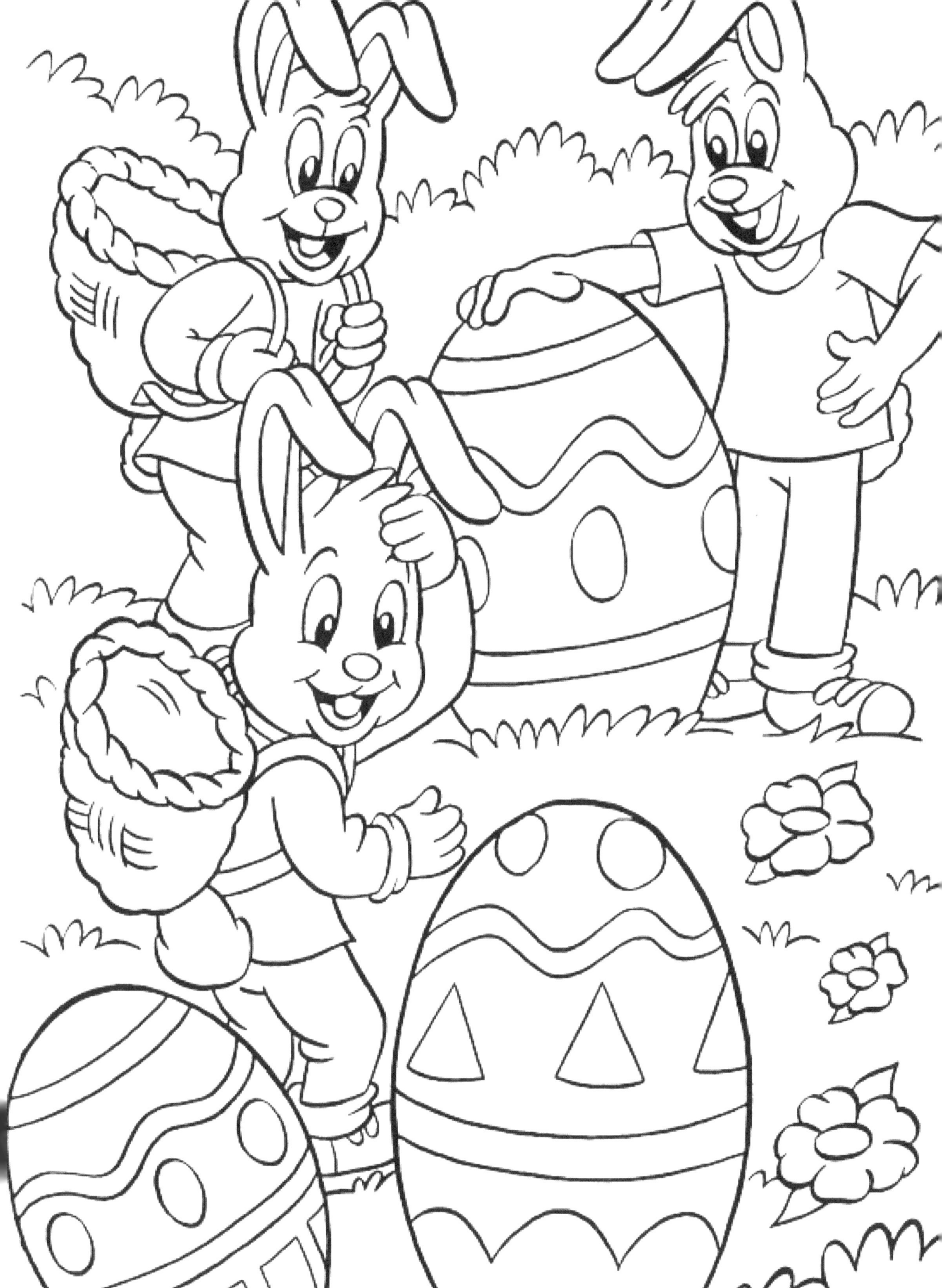

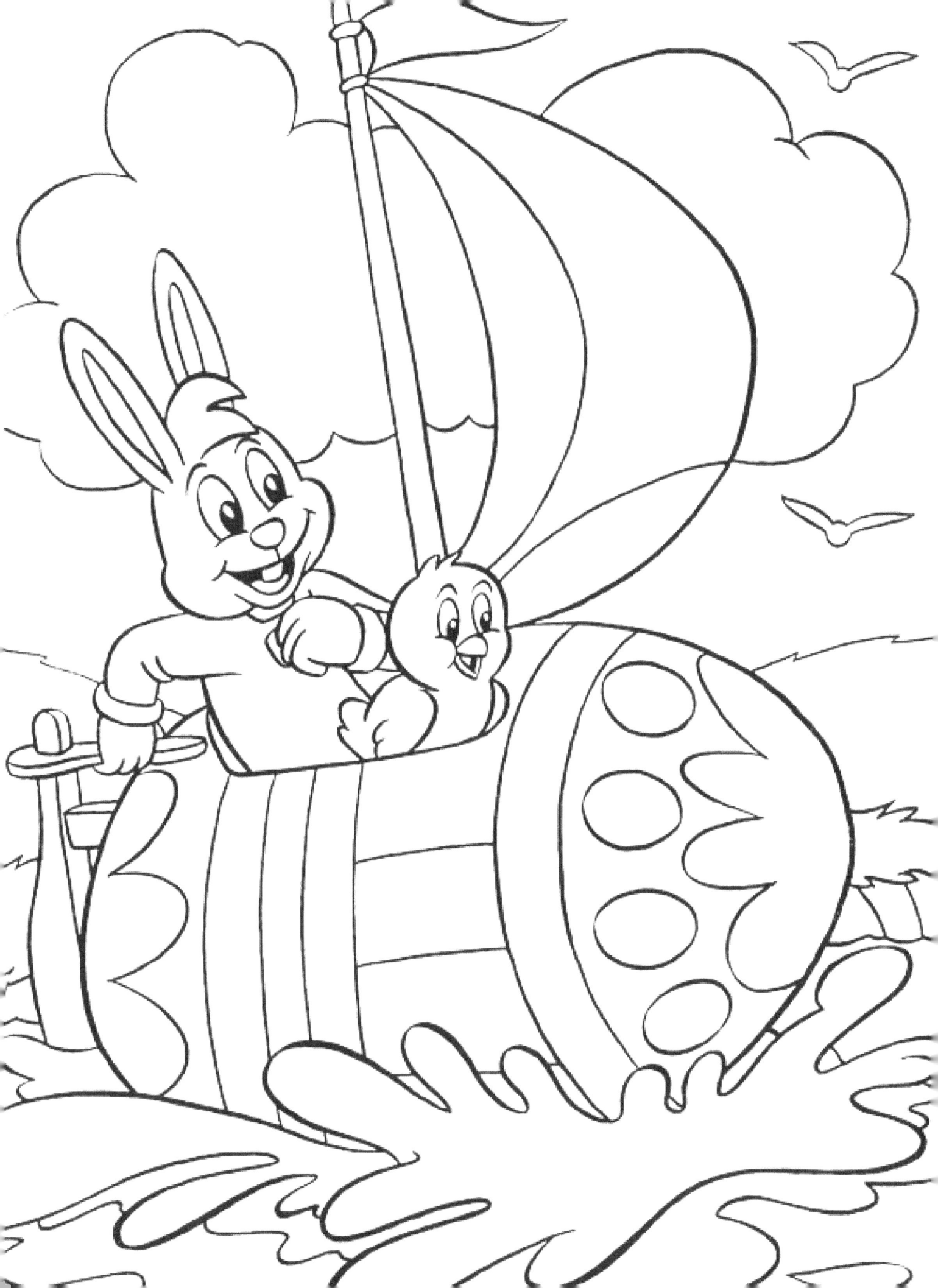

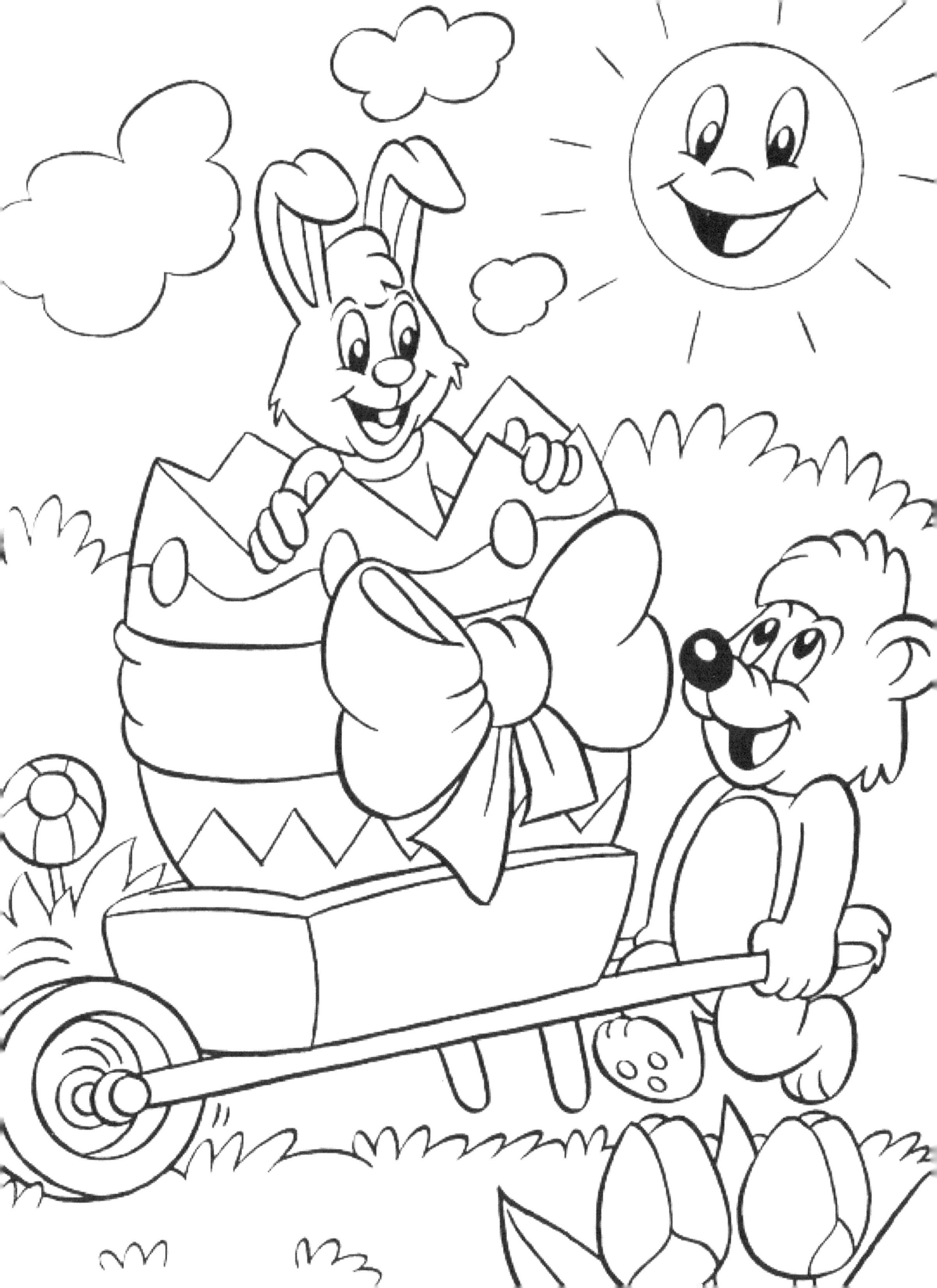

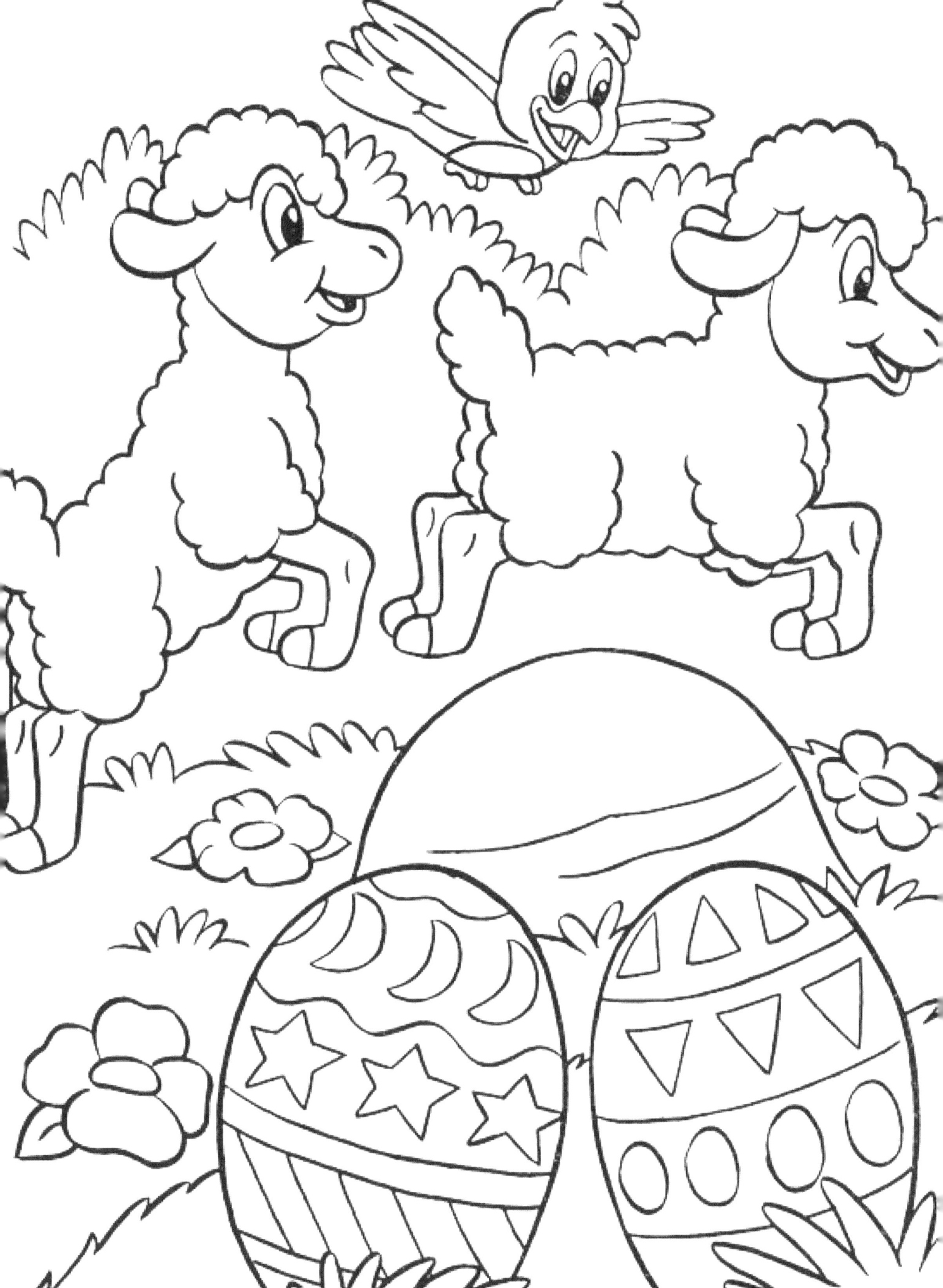

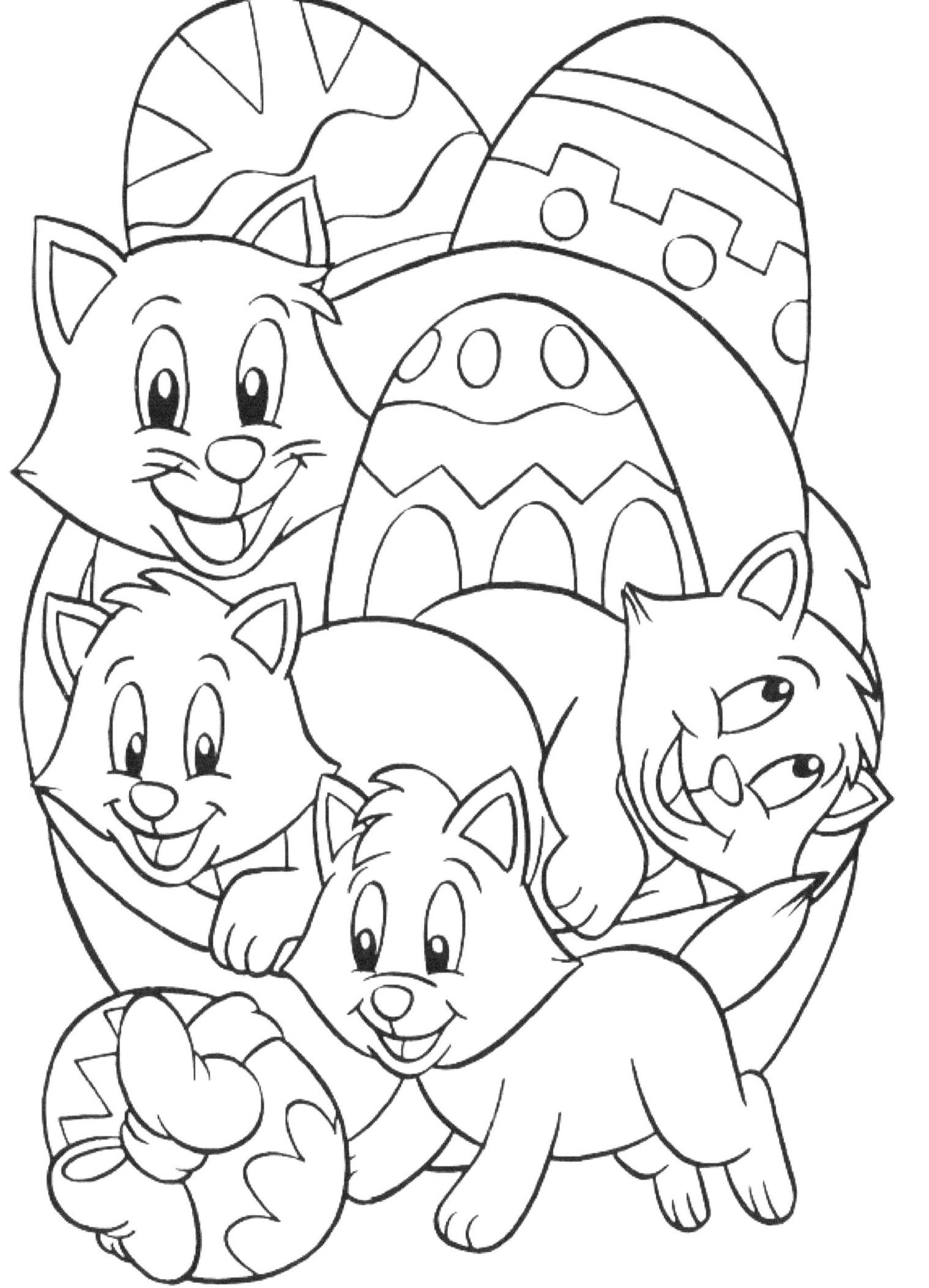

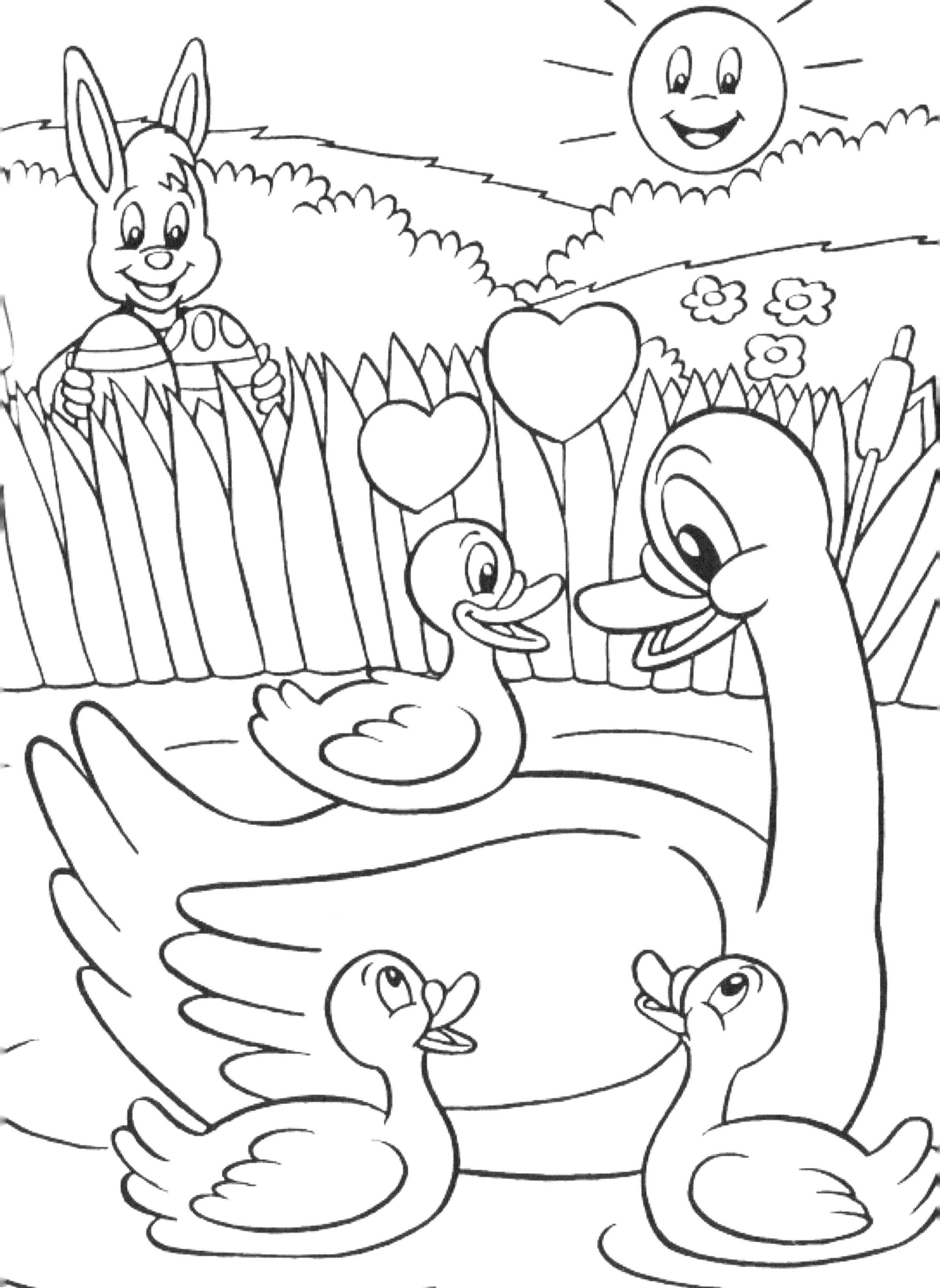

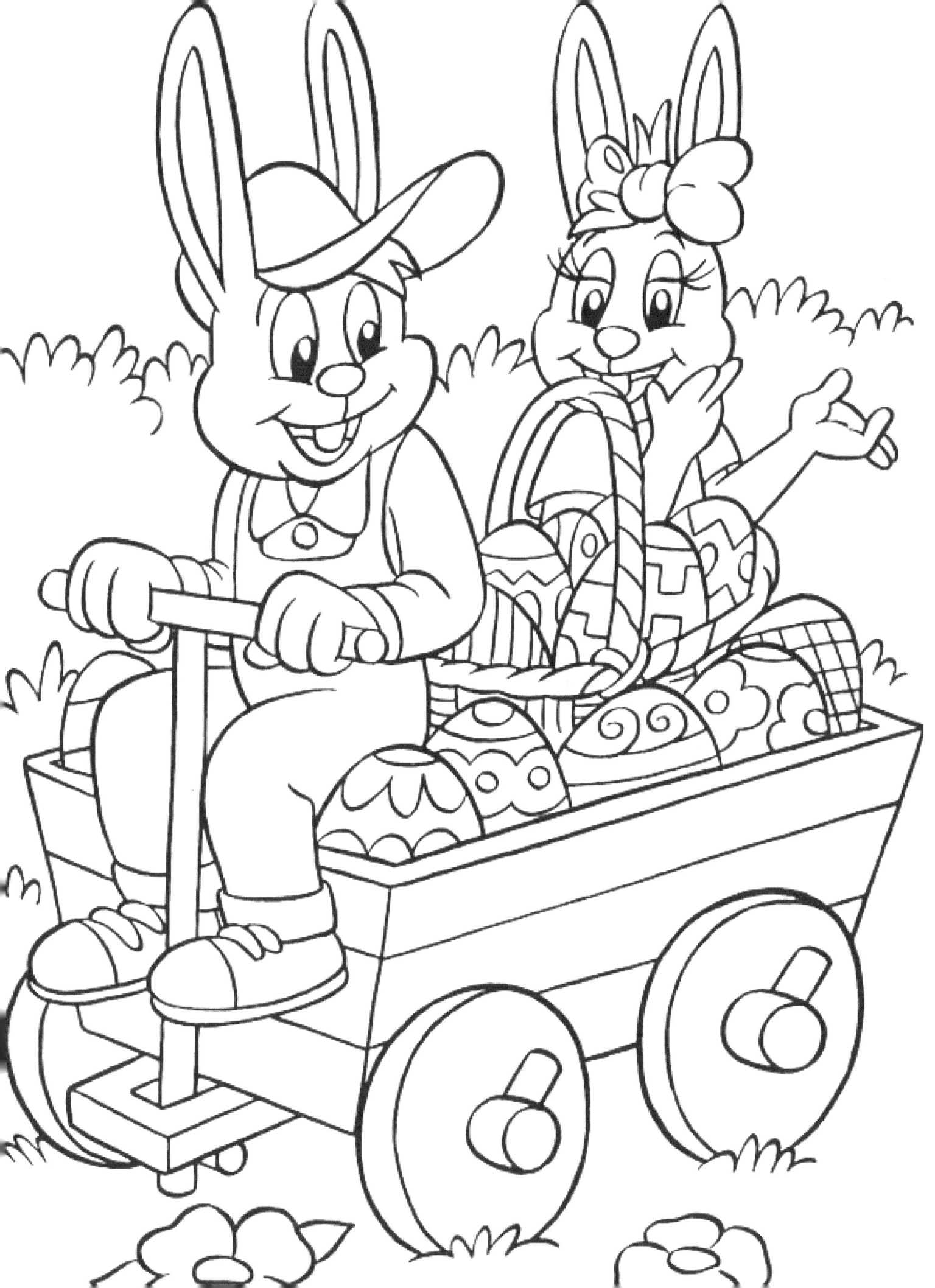

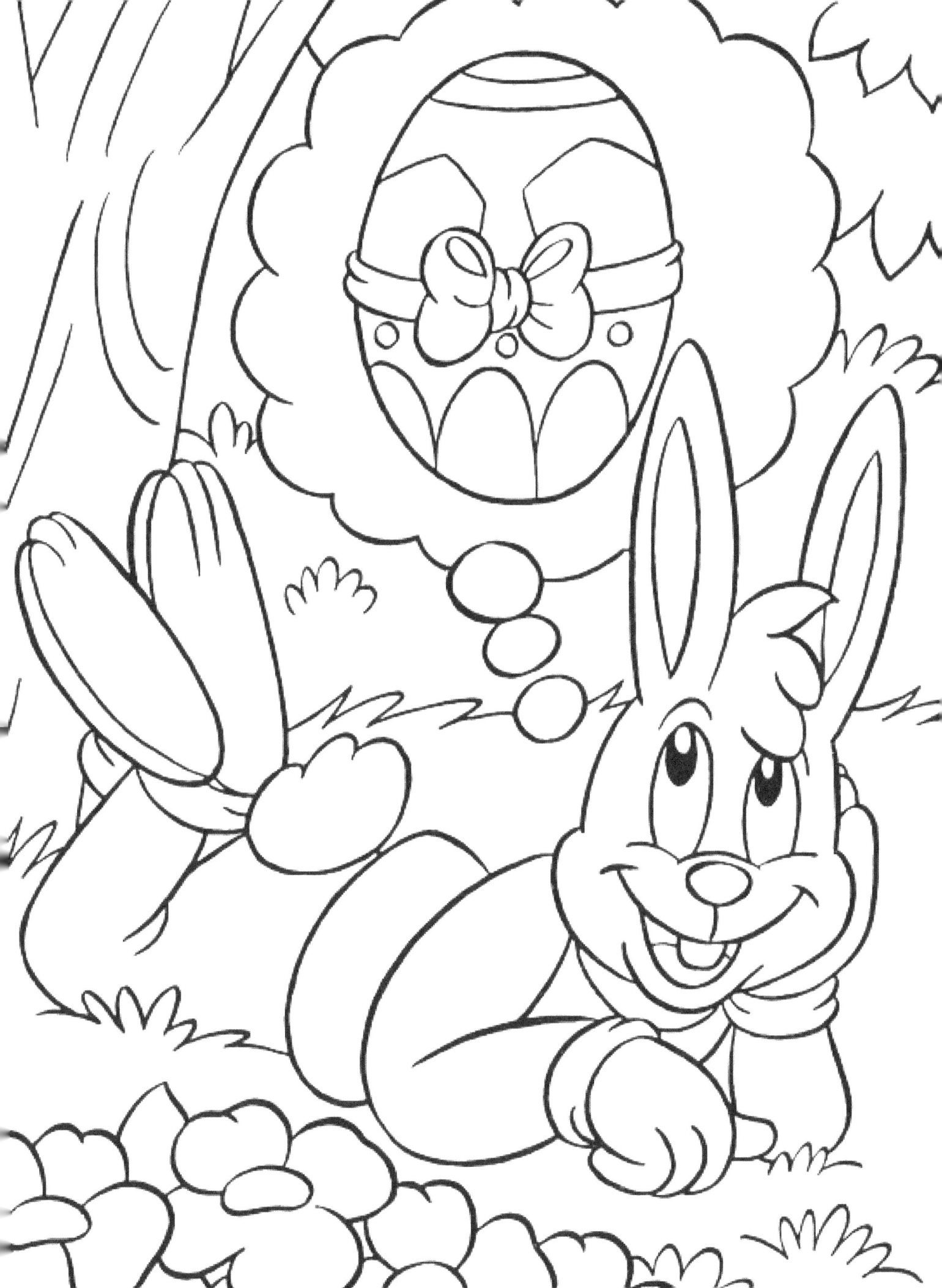

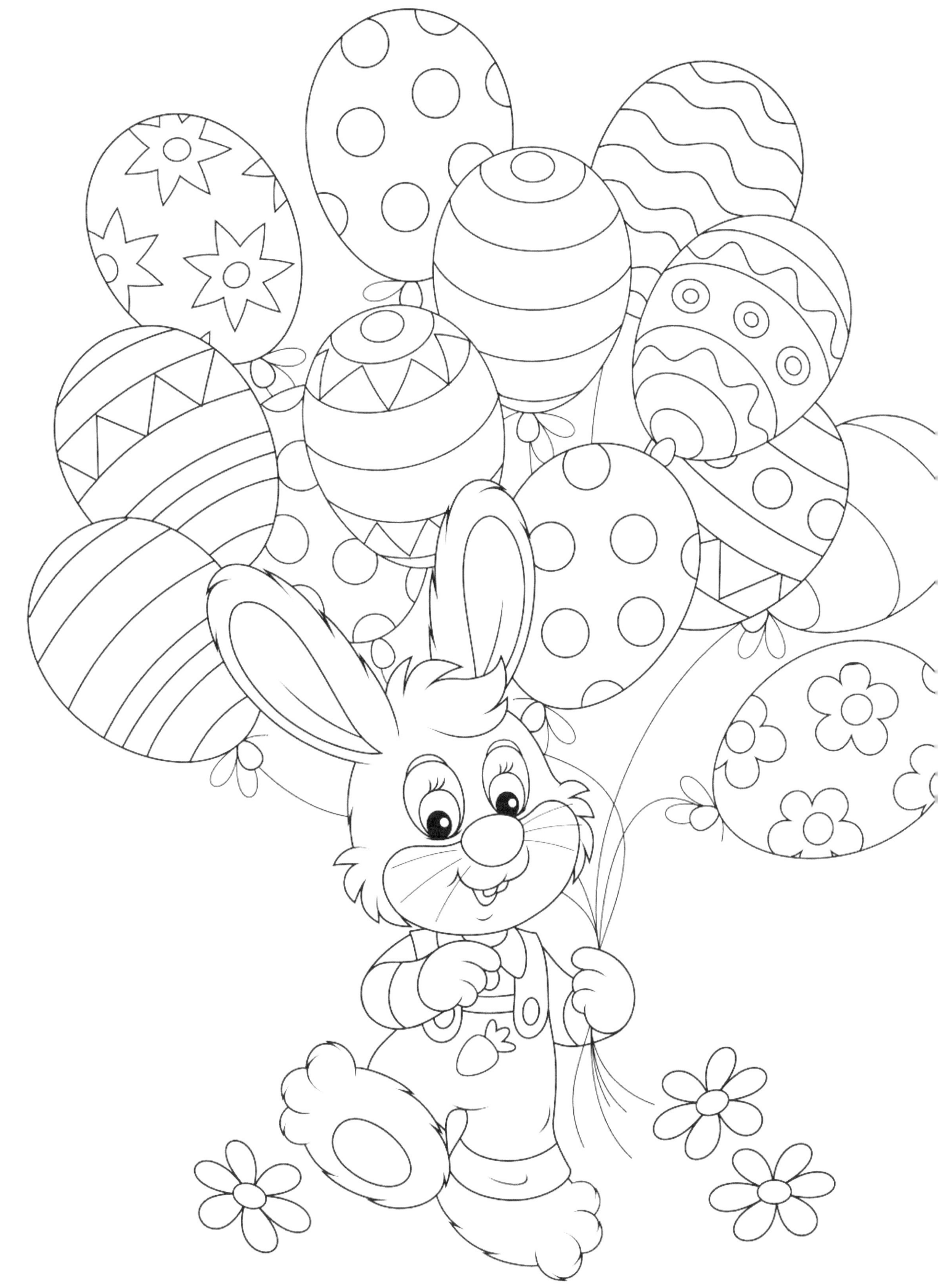

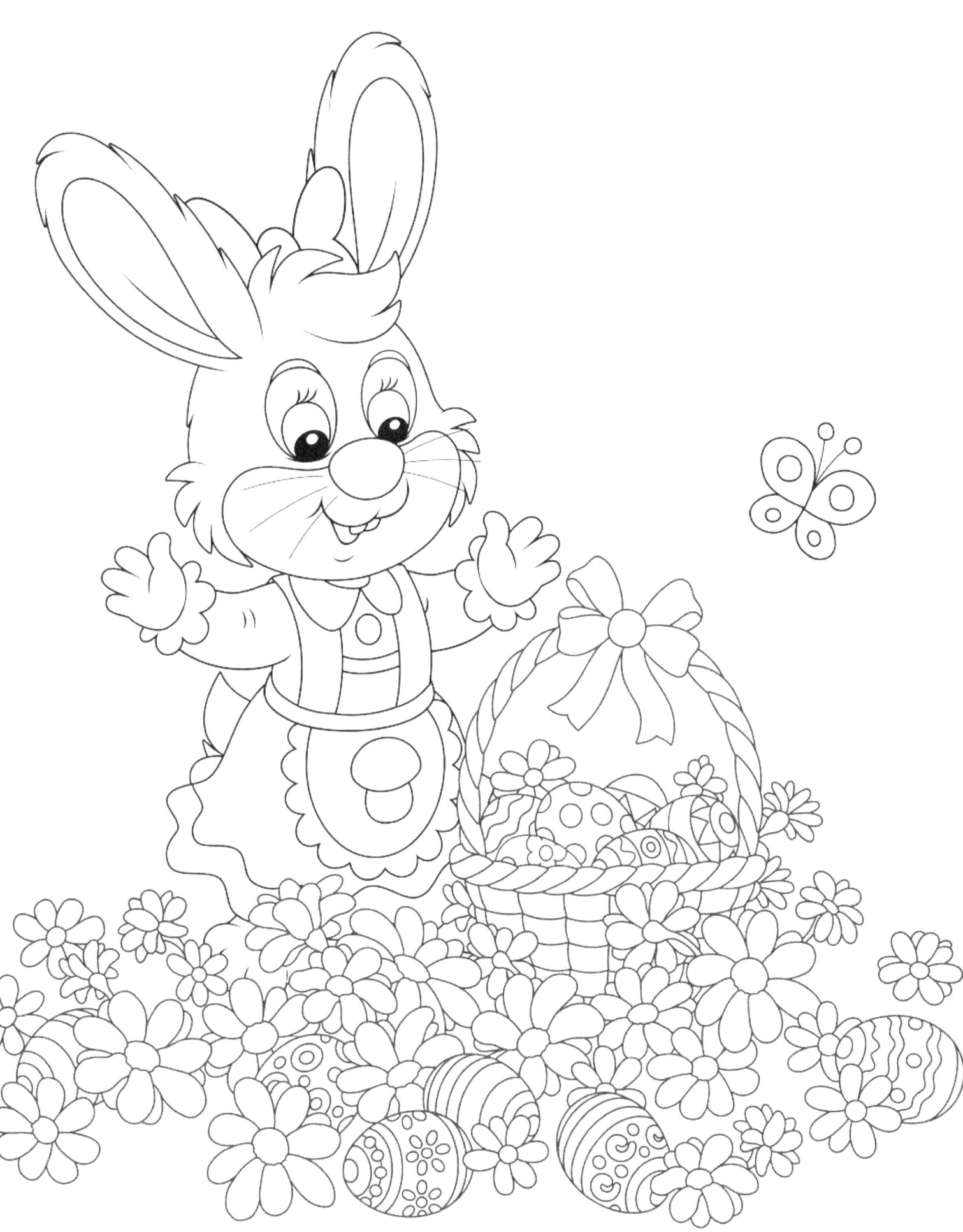

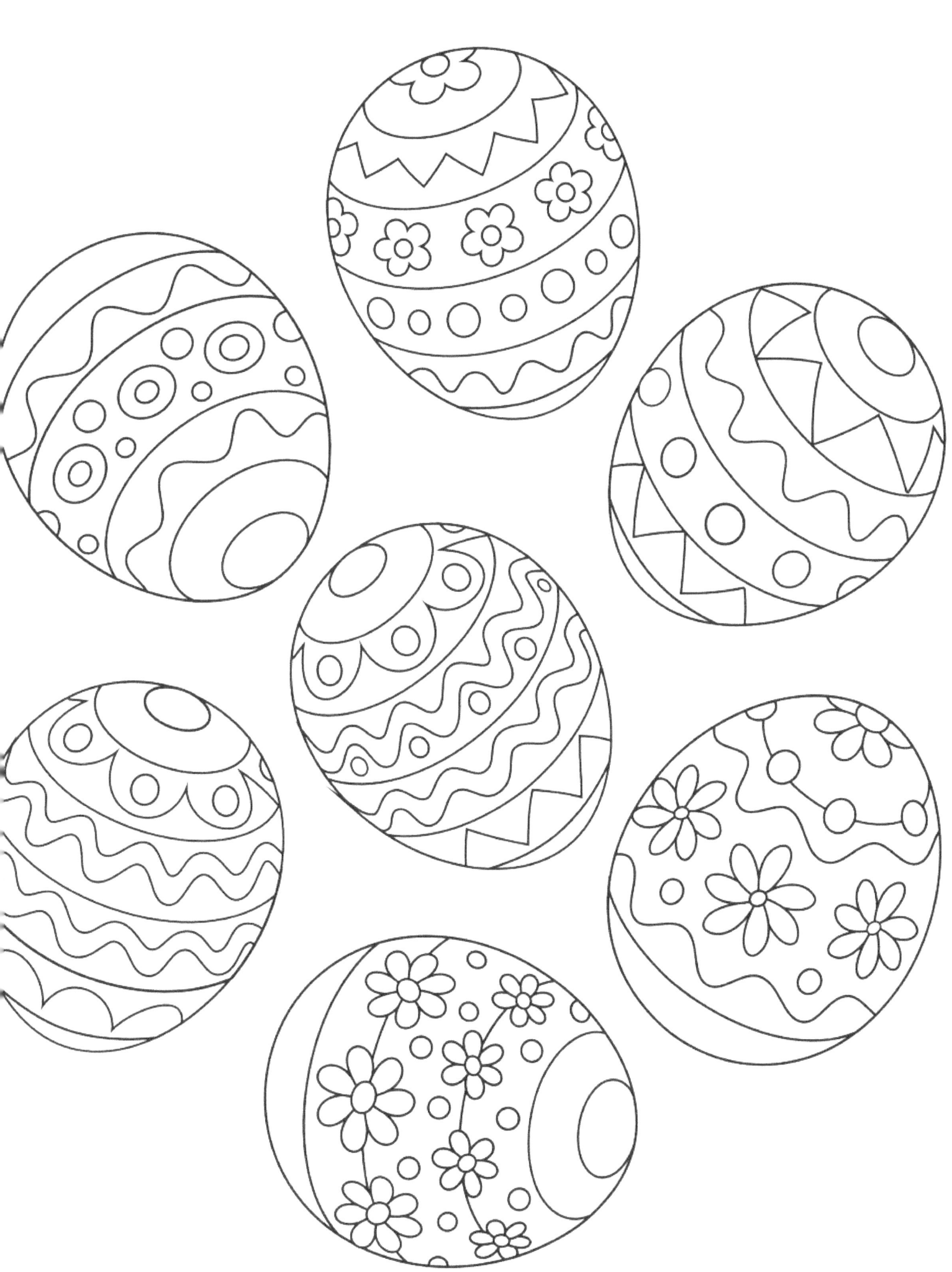

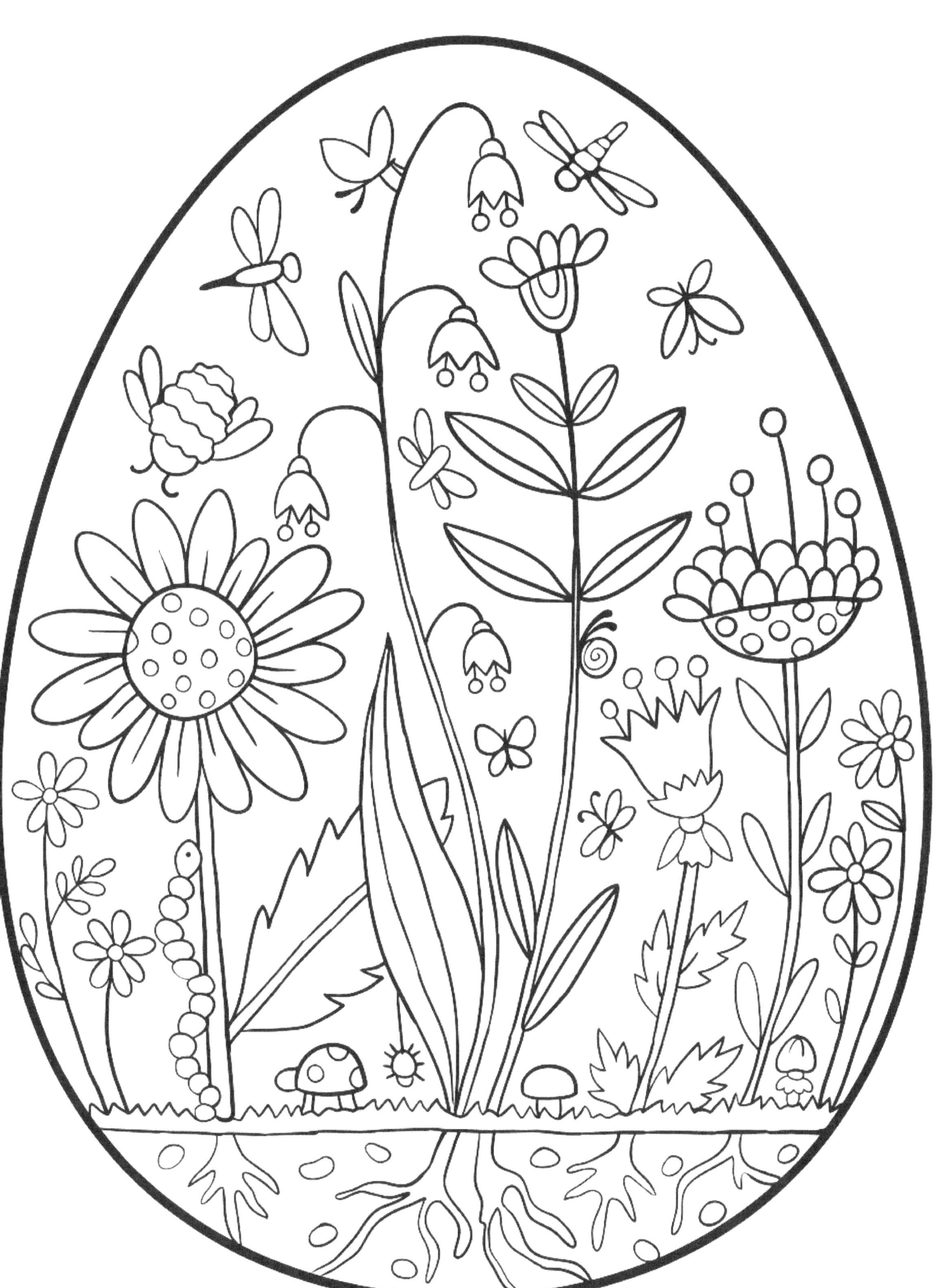

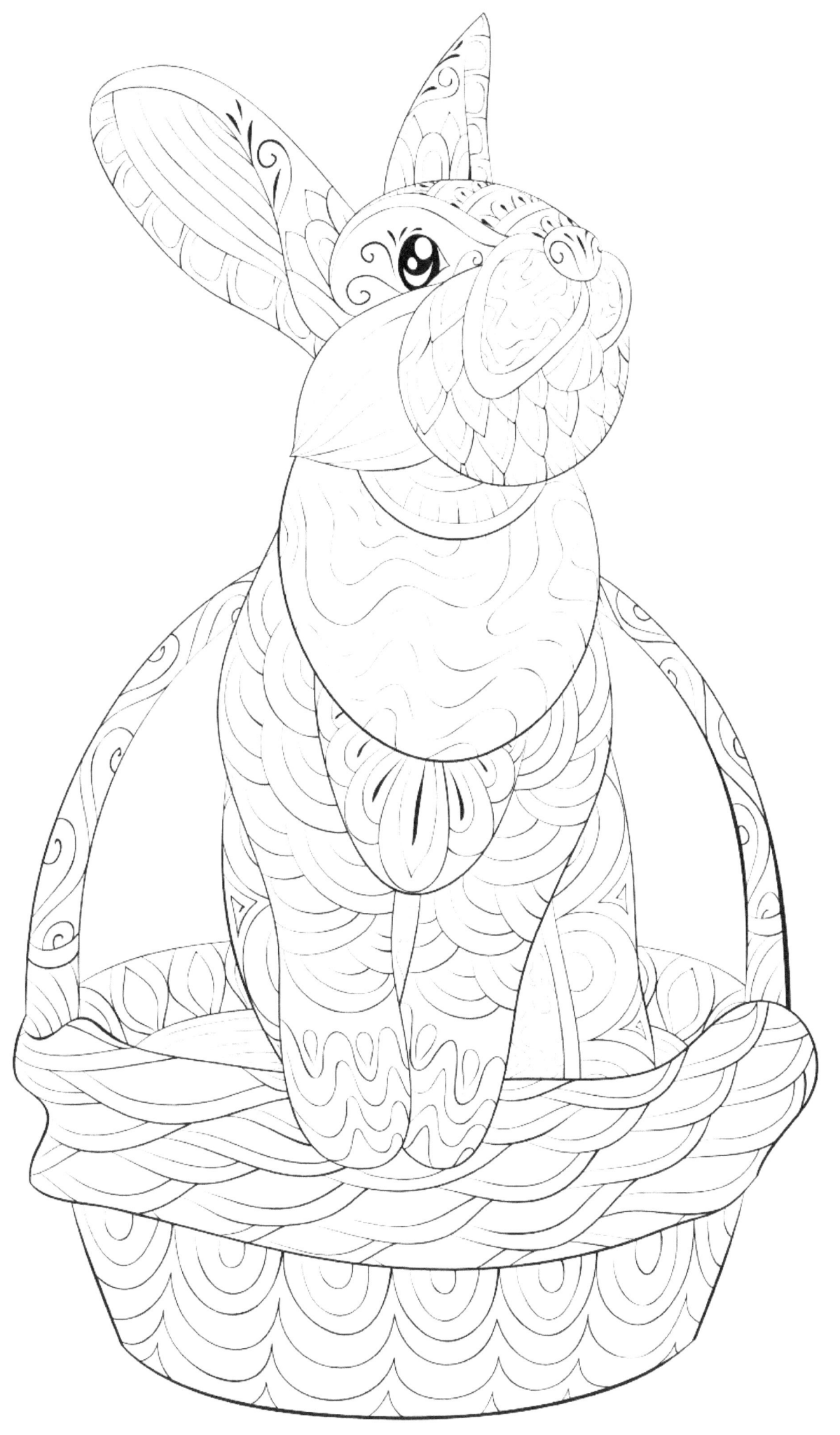

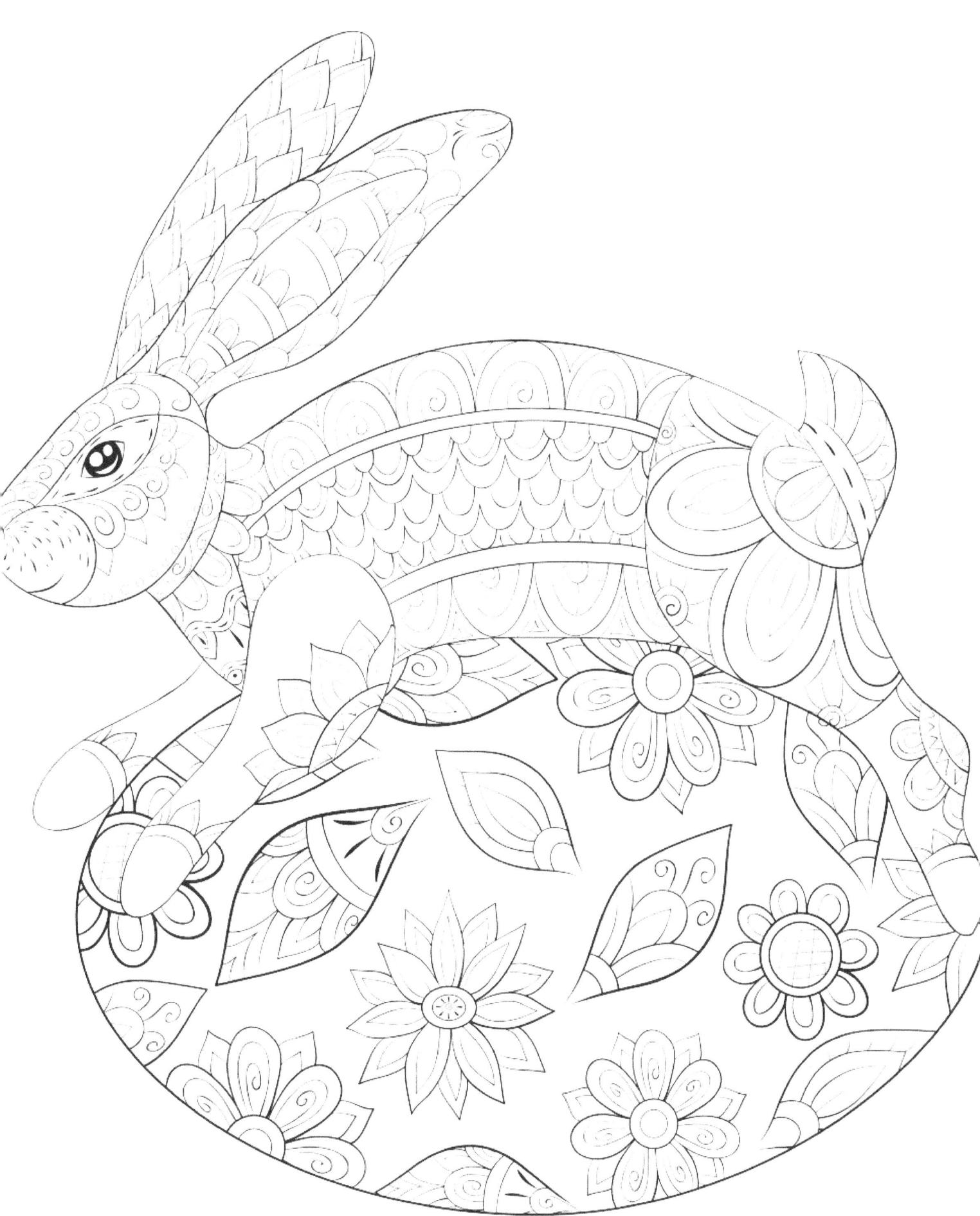

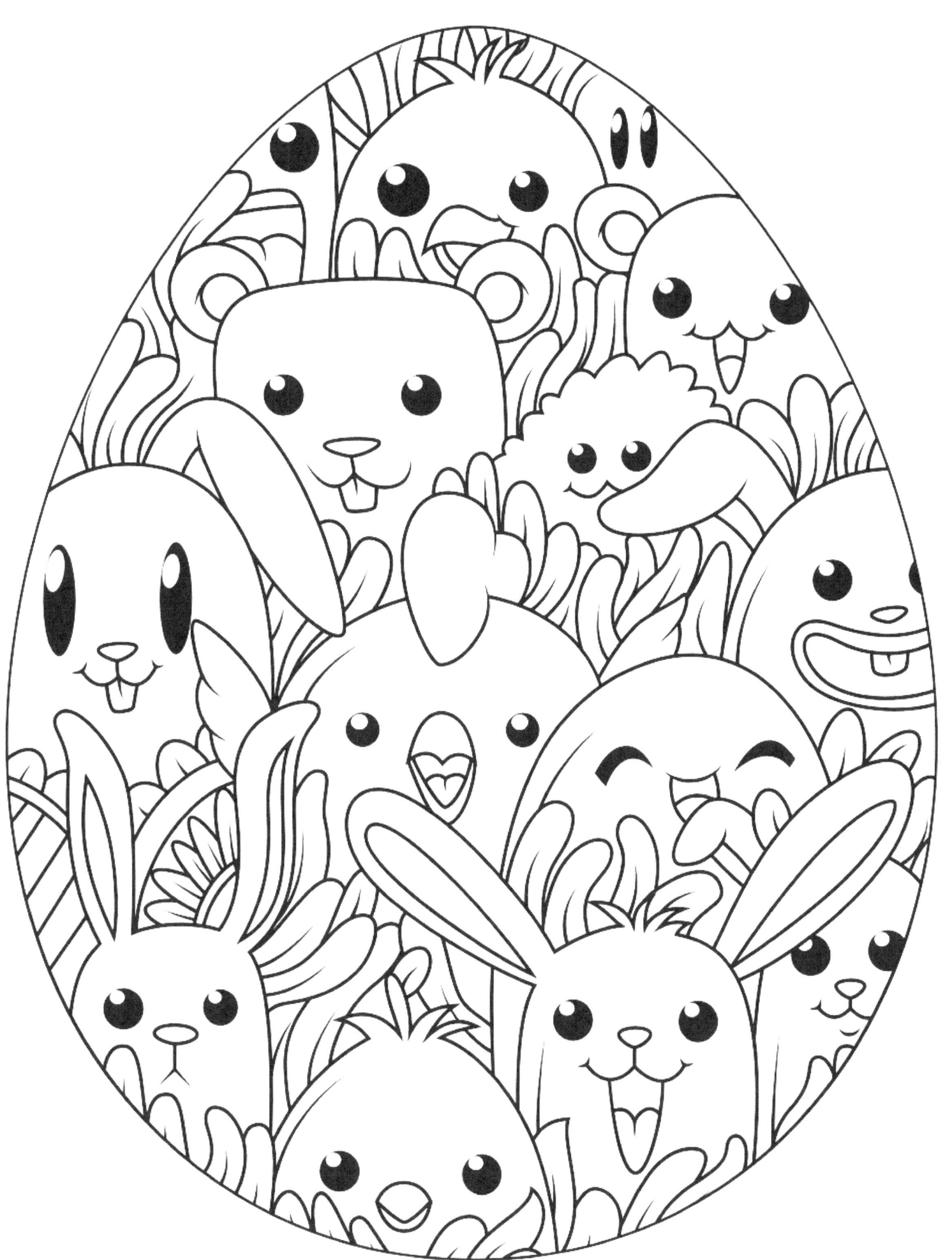

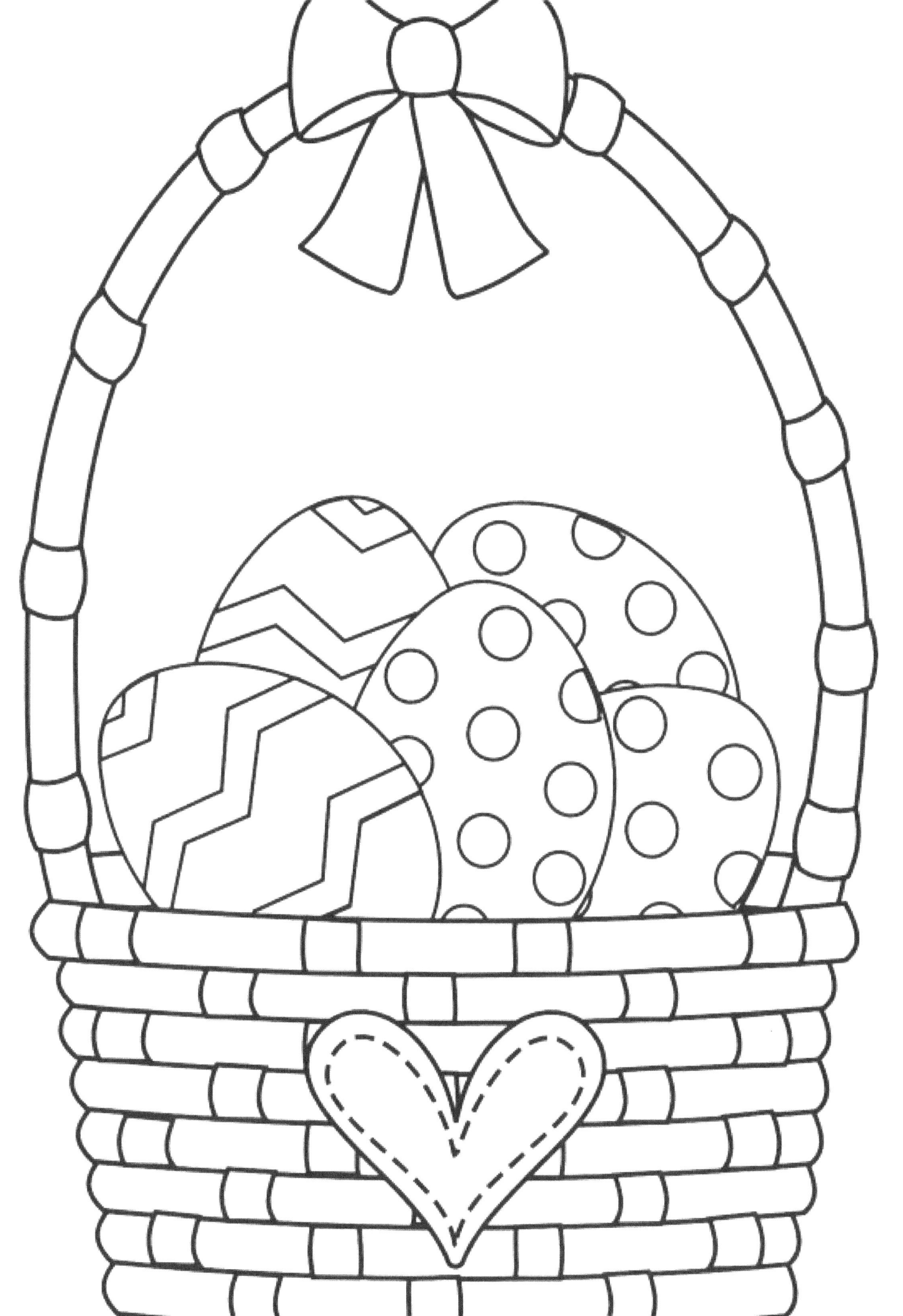

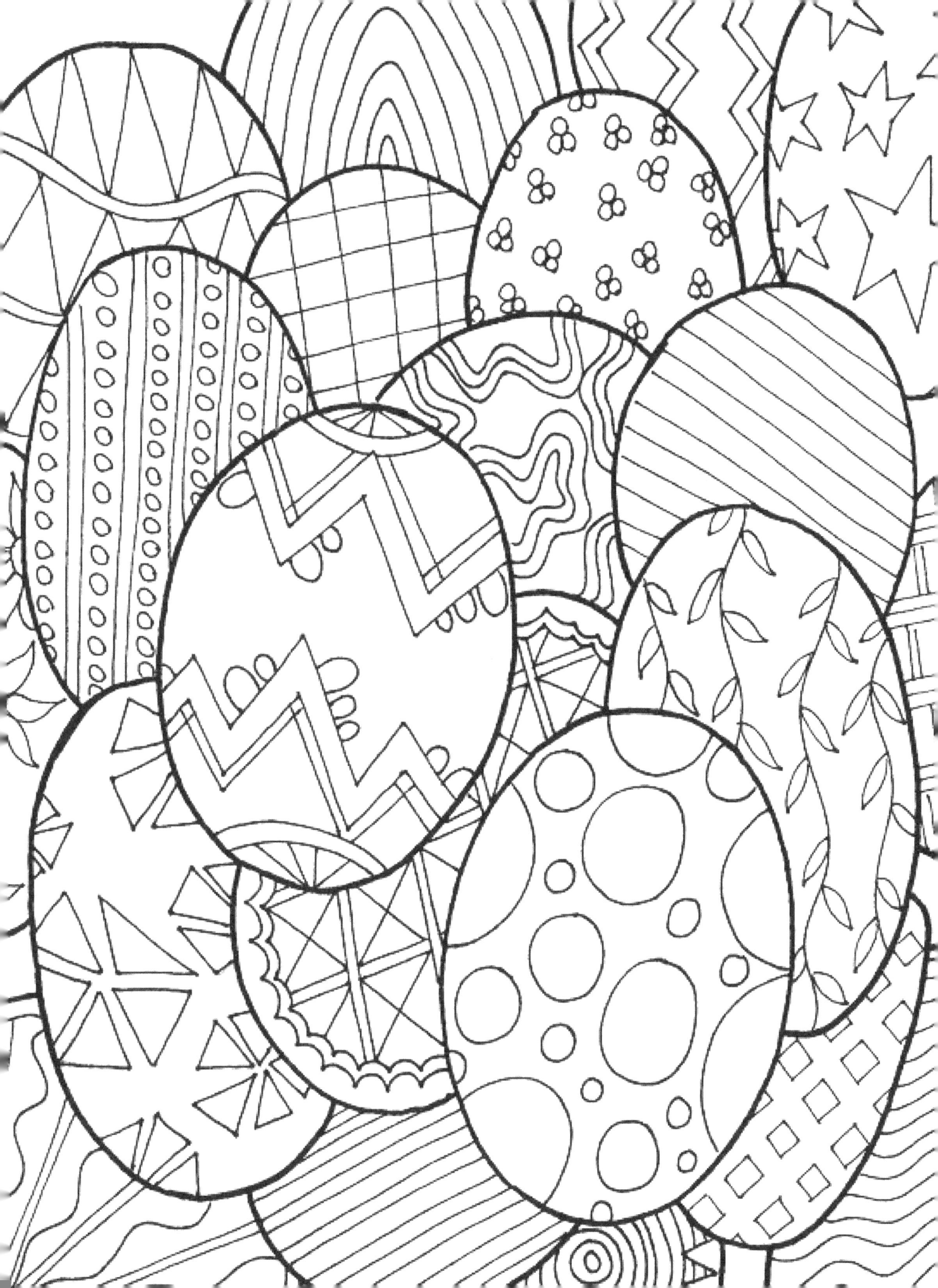

www.ingramcontent.com/pod-product-compliance
Lightning Source LLC
Chambersburg PA
CBHW081001220526
45467CB00008B/2650